Proposing Empirical Research

A Guide to the Fundamentals

Mildred L. Patten

Pyrczak Publishing

P.O. Box 39731 • Los Angeles, CA 90039

Editorial assistance provided by Sharon Young, Brenda Koplin, Cheryl Alcorn, Randall R. Bruce, Elaine Fuess, and Ron Matossian.

Cover design by Robert Kibler and Larry Nichols.

Printed in the United States of America.
10 9 8 7 6 5 4 3 2 1   DOC   05 04 03 02 01 00 99

ISBN 1-884585-25-6

Contents

Introduction

This book was written for students who are writing their first proposals for empirical research. Some students will be doing this as part of a culminating undergraduate course such as a senior research seminar. Others will be required to write one as a class project at the graduate level. Still others will have their first experience when they are required to prepare a proposal for their thesis or dissertation research. Ideally, such students should have taken at least one course in research methods and statistics or should be taking such course(s) concurrently while using this book.

Organization

Part A of this book is designed to help students select a problem area and develop tentative research questions, purposes, or hypotheses. In Part B, they are encouraged to reevaluate and refine them in light of the literature on their topics, relevant theories, and the feasibility of execution of their ideas. These activities should be conducted with considerable care and with an open mind since an idea a student has for research at the beginning of this process may prove to be unsuitable when fully considered in light of all the material in these two parts of the book.

In Part C, students are reminded of the major approaches to research (i.e., types of research) and are encouraged to select a suitable type. Sometimes the type of research selected (e.g., qualitative) has implications for how research purposes, questions, or hypotheses are conceptualized and stated. Hence, some students will want to further refine and tweak their research ideas after considering this material.

In Part D, students are shown how to organize and evaluate the literature they have collected in anticipation of the writing process.

The remaining parts of this book present guidelines for writing various components of a standard research proposal. Here students will find short examples that illustrate important writing techniques.

Sample Proposals

Two sample proposals are included near the end of this book. They are *not* presented as "ideal" proposals since any proposal that is a model of excellence for one purpose (e.g., as a project for a senior undergraduate seminar) may fall far short for another purpose (e.g., seeking major funding for research from a government agency). Instead, they are presented as examples of solid proposals that are consistent with the major recommendations in this book. Students and instructors may react to the proposals in classroom discussions. For example, instructors may wish to point out which parts of the sample proposal are written in a manner suitable for the specific purpose for which students are writing a proposal and which parts need more (or less) explication and detail.

Benefits of Writing a Solid Proposal

Of course, a solid, well-formulated proposal is needed in order to obtain approval for undertaking the proposed research. In addition, a proposal serves as an informal contract since those who approve the proposal are agreeing that if the research is executed as planned, the research will be approved when presented in a research report, thesis, or dissertation. To avoid misunderstandings, this "contract," like all others, should be as explicit and specific as possible—even if the proposed research is "exploratory" or "qualitative." Finally, a solid research proposal can serve as the framework for writing the final research report. For example, if a full-fledged literature review is written for the proposal, it might be used as the literature review in the research report.

Cautionary Notes

Students who are writing a proposal under the supervision of an instructor should seek feedback throughout the process, especially while selecting a research problem and formulating research purposes, questions, or hypotheses. Writing a complete proposal without such feedback is inherently dangerous and could result in rejection of the entire work.

It is important to note that this book presents a framework and guidelines for preparing a standard proposal *as envisioned by this author*. As in any type of writing, there may be legitimate differences of opinion. Students should defer to their instructors when this occurs.

Communicating with Me

I would love to hear from you and am especially interested in your suggestions for improving this book. You can write to me in care of the publisher at the address on the title page.

Mildred L. Patten

Part A

Getting Started

In this part of the book, you will learn how to identify and evaluate broad problem areas in which you might wish to conduct research. In addition, you will learn how to *combine* variables of different types to form research questions, purposes, and hypotheses.

While some of the exercises in this part ask you to practice writing questions, purposes, and hypotheses, you are strongly urged to avoid making a final selection for your research proposal until after you have also completed Part B of this book, which will help you evaluate your tentative ideas for research in light of broader contexts. To use an analogy, *don't get married yet* to an idea. *Date* several ideas, get to know them well, check out their families, and consider their future prospects. Part B will help you with these activities.

Notes

Topic 1

What Is Empirical Research?

The term *empiricism* refers to making *observations* to obtain knowledge. As part of everyday living, we all make informal observations of the people and things around us, and very often, we use these observations as a basis for making decisions. For example, a teacher may observe that his or her students seem bored and decide to switch to a livelier instructional activity.

The term *empirical research* refers to making *planned* observations. By following careful plans for making observations, we engage in a systematic, thoughtful process that deserves to be called *research*.

First, we need to plan *what to observe*. For example, we might wish to observe boredom in the classroom. What other variables should we plan to observe in order to aid in our understanding of boredom? Maybe we should consider skill areas such as math versus creative drawing. Maybe we should consider teaching styles or the match between each student's abilities and the instructional materials that are assigned to him or her. The possibilities are almost endless, so a researcher needs to select those that seem most promising.

Second, we need to plan *whom to observe*. For example, to study boredom in the classroom, we would plan what types of students to observe (e.g., ele-

mentary and/or secondary, middle-class and/or lower socioeconomic students, and so on).

Third, we need to plan *how to observe*. How will we measure boredom (as well as the other variables that might be related to boredom)? Should we ask students directly if they are bored using a questionnaire? By interviewing them? Should we observe the expressions on their faces and infer whether students are bored? If so, who will make the observations, and on what basis will they make the inferences (i.e., what types of facial expressions will be counted as indicating boredom)?

Next, we need to plan *when to observe*. Observations made on a hot Friday afternoon might yield very different results than those made on a clear spring morning.

Finally, we should *plan how to analyze the data* and interpret them. Will we calculate the percentage of students who appear bored while participating in cooperative group activities versus how many appear this way when working individually as they answer questions on worksheets? Will we try to correlate boredom with other variables such as socioeconomic status?

In this book, you will learn how to write a formal research proposal in which all these elements are addressed.

Exercise for Topic 1

Directions: If you already have some ideas for empirical research projects, briefly describe them below. If possible, describe two or more (using additional sheets of paper, if necessary). The ideas you write here will give you talking points for classroom discussions and should be thought of as only tentative, first stabs at the task of preparing a research proposal. As you work through this book, you will probably decide to greatly modify or even abandon your responses to this exercise in favor of more suitable ones.

First Set of Ideas:

1. *What* might you observe?

    The main variable (e.g., boredom in the classroom) is:

    Other variables (e.g., teaching styles) are:

2. *Whom* might you observe?

3. *How* might you observe your main variable (e.g., a test, an interview)?

4. *When* might you make the observations?

Second Set of Ideas:

1. *What* might you observe?

    The main variable (e.g., boredom in the classroom) is:

    Other variables (e.g., teaching styles) are:

2. *Whom* might you observe?

3. *How* might you observe your main variable (e.g., a test, an interview)?

4. *When* might you make the observations?

Topic 2
Identifying Broad Problem Areas

Most beginning students should identify two or three broad problem areas in which they might wish to conduct research. These are broad areas in which many different types of specific research projects may be undertaken. Examples that illustrate what is meant by "broad problem area" are:

- HIV/AIDS prevention
- Alcohol abuse
- Homelessness

One source of ideas for broad problem areas is textbooks that you used in previous courses. Often, the authors will point out areas in which there is controversy or areas that are not fully fleshed out. For example, in the first chapter of his textbook on educational and psychological measurement, Thorndike[1] identifies "some current issues in measurement," which include "testing minority individuals" and "invasion of privacy." In a later chapter, he discusses "current and emerging issues" in the assessment of exceptional children. In yet another chapter, he discusses "problems with personality and interest measures." In each of these sections, the textbook author identifies several broad areas in need of additional research.

Other sources that may help in the identification of a broad problem area are:

- Lecture notes from previous courses.
- Review and reference publications such as the *Encyclopedia of Educational Research*, which contains 2,701 articles organized under 16 broad headings.[2] The articles cover broad areas such as AIDS education, education of pregnant and parenting teenagers, and athletics in higher education.
- "Signature" publications of major professional associations such as the *American Psychologist* published by the American Psychological Association, which carries articles of broad interest to psychologists (as opposed to research journals that carry reports on narrowly defined research).
- Journals that specialize in reviews of research such as *Psychological Bulletin*. Typically, these reviews provide a synthesis of research in a variety of problem areas.
- Discussions with professors, especially those who might be serving on your thesis or dissertation committee.
- Discussions with employers and colleagues.

In the next topic, we'll consider the evaluation of the problem areas you will identify in the exercise for this topic.

---

[1] Thorndike, R. M. (1997). *Measurement and Evaluation in Psychology and Education* (6th ed.). Columbus, OH: Merrill.

[2] Most academic fields have encyclopedias, dictionaries, and/or "handbooks" that summarize research in broad areas. Consult with your reference librarian to see if these are available in your discipline.

Exercise for Topic 2

Directions: List two or three broad problem areas in your field of study in which you might be interested in conducting research. For each, indicate what brought the area to your attention (e.g., textbooks, personal experience, suggestions from others) and rate the degree of your interest in the area on a scale from 1 to 5.

First Problem Area:

1. What brought this area to your attention?

2. How interested are you in this area?

        Very interested   5   4   3   2   1   Not at all interested

Second Problem Area;

1. What brought this area to your attention?

2. How interested are you in this area?

        Very interested   5   4   3   2   1   Not at all interested

Third Problem Area:

1. What brought this area to your attention?

2. How interested are you in this area?

        Very interested   5   4   3   2   1   Not at all interested

Topic 3
Evaluating Broad Problem Areas

Each of the broad problem areas you identified in the Exercise for Topic 2 should now be evaluated. Get feedback from professors, other students, and colleagues. If you are proposing research for a thesis or dissertation, you will want to consider very carefully the interests of the professors who might serve on your committee. If you fail to follow this advice, you might become an "orphan" with no one especially interested in giving you that extra measure of help you inevitably will need at some point in your work.[1]

Other important criteria for evaluating a broad problem area include:

1. Is the problem area in the mainstream of your field of study?

Beginners should consider working in the mainstream because they normally will have a better academic background on mainstream issues. Also, it will be easier for them to locate faculty and other students to help them with mainstream issues. For example, the broad problem area of "homelessness" is more of a mainstream issue for a social work major than a nursing major—although individuals in both professions work with homeless individuals.

2. Is there a substantial body of literature on the problem area?[2]

At first, you might be tempted to think that an area with a substantial body of literature is probably an area in which researchers have exhausted most of the interesting research possibilities. However, the reverse is almost always true: As an area becomes more well-researched, new and *more interesting* facets often emerge. As one researcher builds on the research of another, complex layers of information and data become available that reveal its complexity—suggesting additional promising lines of research.

3. Is the problem area timely?

Timely issues are more likely to be of interest to potential readers of your research. In addition, doing research on them is more likely to advance your career and lead to funding opportunities for your research. Try to distinguish between timely areas (on which there typically will be at least some published research and calls by professionals for more research) and merely fashionable areas that will fade when tomorrow's newspaper headlines are different from today's.

---

[1] When you approach professors with a broad problem area, some of them might want to dive into the thick of things and ask you for your specific research purposes or hypotheses. If this happens, explain that you are not at that stage yet—that you're just considering broad areas and trying to identify faculty who might be interested.

[2] At this point in your academic career, you probably know how to search the major computerized databases of literature in your academic area. For those who do not, Appendix A describes the basics of this process.

Exercise for Topic 3

Directions: Rewrite the names of the three problem areas you identified in the Exercise for Topic 2. Then briefly evaluate each one.

First Problem Area:

1. Is the problem area in the mainstream of your field of study? Explain.

2. Is there a substantial body of literature on the problem area? Explain.

3. Is the problem area timely? Explain.

Second Problem Area:

1. Is the problem area in the mainstream of your field of study? Explain.

2. Is there a substantial body of literature on the problem area? Explain.

3. Is the problem area timely? Explain.

Third Problem Area:

1. Is the problem area in the mainstream of your field of study? Explain.

2. Is there a substantial body of literature on the problem area? Explain.

3. Is the problem area timely? Explain.

Topic 4
Identifying and Combining Variables

To narrow a broad problem area down to a specific research topic, it is helpful to brainstorm a list of *variables* within the area that might be of interest. Most variables can be thought of as belonging to one of three families:

1. *Knowledge.*

Research often focuses on what people know about some topic. Examples of knowledge variables are:

- Knowledge of how HIV is transmitted. (Note that people will differ or *vary* in the amount of this knowledge.)
- Knowledge of community resources for people with HIV.
- Knowledge of treatment options for HIV.

2. *Opinions and Feelings.*

Considerable research deals with this family of variables. Examples are:

- Attitudes toward people with HIV.
- Opinions on federal support for research on HIV.
- Depression among people with children who are HIV positive.

3. *Overt Behavior/Action.*

What people do is also of considerable interest. Examples of variables in this family are:

- Whether people "flee" when someone sitting next to them identifies him- or herself as being HIV positive.
- Frequency of condom use in non-monogamous relationships.
- Use of free clinics by people who are HIV positive.

As you may have already guessed, we combine variables to form interesting research questions. Using two of the *opinions and feelings variables* mentioned above, we could ask:

- Do those with more favorable attitudes toward people with HIV favor more federal support for research on HIV than those with less favorable attitudes?

We can also combine variables across two *different* families of variables and ask research questions such as:

- Do people with more knowledge of how HIV is transmitted have more favorable attitudes toward people with HIV than those with less knowledge?

The exercise for this topic will ask you to brainstorm some variables from each of the three families and try combining them—but do not fall in love yet, and do not get married to a research question! There is still quite a bit of work to do before making the ultimate commitment.

Exercise for Topic 4

Directions: Complete this exercise using one of the broad problem areas you named in your responses to the Exercise for Topic 3. If you are still considering more than one, use additional sheets of paper to complete this exercise for each additional area.

Name a broad problem area here:

1. List at least four *knowledge* variables within the problem area.

2. List at least four *opinions and feelings* variables within the problem area.

3. List at least four *overt behavior/action* variables within the problem area.

4. Combine two variables from *one family of variables* into a research question.

5. Combine two variables from *two different families of variables* into a research question.

Topic 5
Identifying Treatment Variables

When researchers give treatments such as an aspirin a day to one group and a placebo to another, they create a variable known as an *independent variable*. The people in the study *vary* (or differ) because of what the researcher has done to them. (Those in one group have thinner blood than those in the other because of the thinning effects of aspirin.) The formal name of such a study is an *experiment*.

As you plan your research, you will need to decide whether you wish to conduct an experiment. To make this decision, consider possible treatments you might give to affect the variables you named in your responses to questions 1 through 3 in the Exercise for Topic 4. In other words, consider what treatments you might give to affect *knowledge*, or *opinions and feelings*, or *overt behavior/action*.

At first, some students think that conducting an experiment is inherently more difficult than conducting a nonexperimental study. Yet, the literature is full of simple, revealing experimental studies. For example:

A researcher prepared two versions of a resume. The two were identical except that one version stated "Health condition: Perfect" and the other stated "Health condition: HIV+." Different versions were mailed to different potential employers, and the number of positive responses from employers was logged.

As you can see, the potential employers were "treated" with different versions of the resume. Note that the effort to conduct the experiment was not greater than the effort it would take to conduct an opinion survey by mail.

As you consider potential treatments, look for ones that might produce a big bang—that is, those that have a good chance of being highly effective. For example, tutoring children (the treatment) for a few hours would be unlikely to produce much of an effect on a nationally standardized math test. However, a few hours of tutoring on the addition of simple fractions might produce a big gain on a test that measures only this particular math skill. Of course, it is sometimes hard to guess in advance if a particular treatment will produce a big effect, which is why it is important to get feedback from people who have professional experience in conducting experiments.

Although the exercise for this topic will ask you to identify some potential independent variables, note that you should immerse yourself in the literature on the topic that you eventually select to identify which treatments have already been tried and how effective they have been before making a final selection.

Exercise for Topic 5

PART A: Directions: This exercise is for practice only. If you will be conducting an experiment, you will want to explore the research literature carefully to identify promising treatments.

1. Select one of the *knowledge* variables that you listed in response to question 1 in Exercise 4 and write it here:

   Name an *independent variable* (i.e., treatments) that might increase the knowledge.

2. Select one of the *opinions and feelings* variables that you listed in response to question 2 in Exercise 4 and write it here:

   Name an *independent variable* (i.e., treatments) that might change the opinions and feelings.

3. Select one of the *overt behavior/action* variables that you listed in response to question 3 in Exercise 4 and write it here:

   Name an *independent variable* (i.e., treatments) that might change the overt behavior/action.

PART B: Directions: On the following scale, rate how interested you are in conducting an experiment at this point in your planning. Explain the reason for your rating.

Very interested   5   4   3   2   1   Not at all interested

Topic 6
Considering Demographic Variables

Demographic variables are background characteristics of the participants you will be studying. Many demographics are considered in research in the social and behavioral sciences. Examples are:

- Highest (or current) educational level
- Socioeconomic status
- Age
- Major in school
- Employment status
- Gender

You will want to consider demographics at this point because there probably will be some that you will want to *hold constant* in the study you are planning. For example, you might want to hold gender and educational level constant by studying only women enrolled in college. If so, you will probably want to add this information to your emerging research questions since it will be an important restriction on what you will be studying. For instance, we might pose this question:

- Among female college students, will those with more knowledge of HIV report more abstention from casual sex than those with less knowledge?

Notice the three elements in the question: (1) two demographic variables (gender and educational level) that are held constant, (2) a knowledge variable, and (3) an overt behavior/action variable.

There are three important considerations in selecting demographic variables to hold constant. First, there is the practical matter of what types of people you have access to for research. For example, if you teach fifth-grade students, you may wish to confine yourself to this readily available sample. Second, you should consider the demographic types that are most likely to exhibit the behaviors you wish to observe. For example, college-level students are more likely to be sexually active with multiple partners than middle-aged or elderly people. Thus, they might be a fruitful group with which to conduct a study on AIDS prevention. Third, you should consider whether holding a demographic variable constant will help you simplify your study so that it is manageable given your resources. For example, a study on AIDS prevention using only males or only females is inherently simpler than one with both males and females.

Note that important demographic variables that you do *not* hold constant will need to be described in your research report. For example, you may study college-level women who vary in age. You will want to plan to collect information on age so that you can describe this demographic characteristic in your research report.

Exercise for Topic 6

Directions: Keep in mind that your responses to this exercise are for practice only. Final selection of one or more research questions should take place only after you complete Part B of this book.

1. Rewrite the research question that you wrote for question 4 in the Exercise for Topic 4.

Revise the research question to include reference to one or more demographic variables that might be held constant (e.g., "Among female college students...").

2. Rewrite the research question that you wrote for question 5 in the Exercise for Topic 4.

Revise the research question to include reference to one or more demographic variables that might be held constant (e.g., "Among female college students...").

Topic 7
Writing Purposes and Hypotheses

In Topics 4 through 6, you saw how variables can be combined to form *research questions*. Consider the following example of a research question with two variables (free-floating anxiety and success in quitting smoking) plus a demographic variable (age/adulthood) that is held constant.

- Among adults, is there a relationship between free-floating anxiety and success in quitting smoking?

Sometimes researchers prefer to state a *research purpose* (a statement instead of a question). Using the same variables as in the example above, here is a research purpose:

- The purpose is to explore the relationship between free-floating anxiety and success in quitting smoking.

The choice between stating a research question and a research purpose is largely a matter of personal preference. However, notice that both are neutral regarding the nature of the relationships among variables.

If you are willing to predict the nature of the relationship, you should state a *hypothesis* instead of a research question or purpose because a hypothesis indicates what you *expect* to find. Using the same variables as in the previous examples, here is a research hypothesis:

- Adults who have more free-floating anxiety will be less successful in their attempts to quit smoking than those with less anxiety.

While research questions, purposes, and hypotheses should be reasonably specific, avoid being overly specific about the anticipated statistical outcome. Here is one that is too specific:

- Adults who have more free-floating anxiety will be 55% less successful in quitting smoking than those with less anxiety.

It will be almost impossible for the data to support this hypothesis because there will have to be exactly 55% less (not 54%; not 56%; not any other percentage) for confirmation of the hypothesis. Thus, the hypothesis that says simply that there will be *less success* without quantifying it is superior.

As you consider possible research questions, purposes, and hypotheses, keep in mind that a research proposal may be based on more than one of them. Generally, however, they should be closely related. Here is an example in which there are three related hypotheses:

- Among adults, there is an inverse relationship between success in quitting smoking and:
  1. free-floating anxiety,
  2. depression, and
  3. interpersonal dependency needs.

Exercise for Topic 7

Directions: You should still consider your responses to the following questions as highly tentative. Final selection of research questions, purposes, and hypotheses should not be made until after reading Part B of this book.

1. Rewrite here the research question that you wrote for question 4 in the Exercise for Topic 4:

    Revise the research question so that it is in the form of a *research purpose*:

    Revise the research question so that it is in the form of a *research hypothesis*:

2. Rewrite here the research question that you wrote for question 5 in the Exercise for Topic 4:

    Revise the research question so that it is in the form of a *research purpose*:

    Revise the research question so that it is in the form of a *research hypothesis*:

Part B

A Closer Look at Problem Selection

Having completed Part A of this book, you should have several tentative research questions, purposes, or hypotheses within one or two broad problem areas. In this section, you will be encouraged to consider other possibilities within the problem areas, evaluate them, and make a final selection for your research proposal.

Note that the research questions, purposes, or hypotheses are the *heart* of your proposal. If they are not solid and suitable, your proposal will be unsatisfactory regardless of your excellence in writing the other portions of the proposal.

Notes

Topic 8
Finding Ideas in the Literature

Before making a final selection of research questions, purposes, or hypotheses on which to base your proposal, you should read extensively on the problem area(s) that you have selected. While reading books (especially textbooks) will give you a broad overview, at this point you need to immerse yourself in the specifics of how others have conducted research. These specifics can be found in reports of original research published in academic journals. Such reports (called *research articles*) can be identified electronically. See Appendix A if you are unfamiliar with conducting such searches. Although electronic databases often provide abstracts (summaries) of the articles, it is essential that you obtain copies of the full articles and carefully read them in their entirety.

As you read, pay special attention to *the specific research questions, purposes, or hypotheses* that are stated in the article. Usually these can be found in the paragraph immediately above the heading "Method" in the articles. Ask yourself:

- Are the questions, purposes, or hypotheses similar to ones you have been considering for your research?
- Could any of them be modified to create a new problem that you might wish to investigate?
- Were any of them sufficiently important that a replication of the study is warranted? Would you want to propose a replication (i.e., another study

designed to see if similar results are obtained)? Can you get approval from your instructor to propose a replication? (Note that as a learning exercise, your instructor may want you to propose "original" research rather than a replication.)

You should also pay special attention to the *discussion* sections that appear at the end of most articles. In these discussions, researchers often describe the *limitations* (i.e., weaknesses) of their studies. Ask yourself whether you could propose research without these limitations. If so, you may want to propose a *modified replication* of a study in which you improve on the research methodology.

In their discussions, researchers also often describe *possible directions for future research*. Consider whether any are of sufficient interest to you that you might want to propose research along the lines suggested. These suggestions deserve careful consideration since they are being made by experienced researchers who have conducted publishable research on a topic within your problem area. Contrary to what some beginning students think, most researchers are more than happy to share their best research ideas with others. There is no greater compliment than having others build on one's previous research and having the original research cited as the inspiration.

Exercise for Topic 8

Directions: Read at least three reports of original research (research articles) in one of your problem areas, and answer the following questions.

1. Did the articles help you refine the research questions, purposes, or hypotheses that you have been considering? Explain.

2. Did the articles give you ideas for new research questions, purposes, or hypotheses? Explain.

3. What other benefits, if any, did you get from reading the articles?

4. Do you feel that you are closer to making a final selection of research questions, purposes, or questions to propose as a result of reading the journal articles? Explain.

Topic 9

Considering a Body of Literature

Before making a final selection of research questions, purposes, or hypotheses on which to base your proposal, you should consider the body of literature as a whole. In other words, read all the articles you have collected on your general topic and reflect on them *as a group*. Ask yourself:

- What are the trends in research perspectives *over time*? For instance, does newer research use different conceptualizations than older research? As a general rule, you will want to use the newer conceptualizations unless you have a very good reason for doing otherwise.

- Are there particular lines of research that have been especially fruitful in uncovering important results? Are there unfruitful lines that you will want to avoid?

- Are certain previous studies repeatedly cited by current researchers? If so, this may point you to the historical roots of current lines of research. You will want to read carefully such landmark or classic studies for possible ideas for your proposed research.

- Are there obvious gaps in the body of research literature? For example, have all the researchers used only college women as participants? Do you have access to other groups of women that you might propose to study?

Note that your task in answering these questions will often be made easier by researchers who discuss such issues in their research articles. The following example shows how one researcher summarized trends in the conceptualization of sex differences in cognitive abilities.

Example

The older reviews of cognitive differences tended to view them as individual attributes—either the product of biology or of social learning. This was, however, an oversimplification even for cognitive attributes. ...social context is important even for supposedly internalized skills. For social behavior, it is essential to consider the context in which it is manifest, and this led to changes of emphasis in the way sex differences were conceptualized.... The emphasis had therefore shifted to processes such as gender-stereotypic beliefs and the salience of these beliefs for those people in a given situation. Sex differences were consequently viewed as flexible, context-dependent outcomes of social processes.[1]

As a result of such a historical analysis, someone planning research in the area of sex differences in cognitive abilities would want to consider whether these should be examined within some specific social context. If so, the research questions, purposes, or hypotheses should reflect this by referring to the context (i.e., within a certain social context, certain behaviors will be exhibited).

---

[1] Archer, J. (1996). Sex differences in social behavior: Are the social role and evolutionary explanations compatible? *American Psychologist, 51,* 909–917.

21

Exercise for Topic 9

Directions: After considering the research in your problem area, answer the following questions.

1. Are there changes in the trends in research perspectives over time? Explain. If yes, how will it affect your formulation of research questions, purposes, or hypotheses?

2. Are there lines of research within your area that have been particularly fruitful? Unfruitful?

3. Are certain previous studies repeatedly cited in current research? If yes, have you read these landmark studies? Explain.

4. Have you found any obvious gaps in the research on your topic? Explain. If yes, will you consider proposing research to fill one or more of the gaps? Explain.

Topic 10

Considering Theories

A *theory* is a unified explanation for discrete observations that might otherwise be viewed as unrelated or contradictory. For instance, portions of the helplessness-hopelessness theory of the cognitive origins of depression are described in this example:

Example

> ...anxiety commonly precedes depression and is more likely to occur if negative events are perceived as being uncontrollable (thus promoting a helplessness expectancy). In addition, as the individual becomes increasingly certain that event causes are stable (enduring over time) and global (affecting many life outcomes), he or she should be more likely to become hopeless and to develop symptoms of hopelessness depression. Depression is therefore seen as a progression from anxiety, and the co-occurrence of these mood states corresponds to a transition on the cognitive continuum from helplessness to hopelessness.[1]

This theory has many implications for the study of depression. For example, someone studying the etiology of depression might want to take account of anxiety as a variable in his or her proposed research.

Note that being able to say in a proposal that the proposed research will either test some aspect of a theory or, at least, has its origins in a theory is a good way to help justify the research. This is true because the results are less likely to be viewed as isolated data; instead, they are likely to contribute to a larger context

for understanding behavior. Thus, you will want to consider whether your research questions, purposes, or hypotheses can be related to one or more theories.

Survey textbooks in most content areas usually cover only the most important, well-established theories. However, research on newer theories that are not as established may be more interesting and make more substantial contributions. As you read research articles in your problem area, you are likely to identify such theories. In addition, you might conduct an electronic database search in which you include the term *theory*. For example, a search of *PsycINFO*, the major database in psychology, using the terms "television," "violence" *and* "theory," identified ten research articles, including one that explored the "tainted fruit theory," which leads to the prediction "that warning labels will increase interest in violent programs." Of course, those who conduct future research in this area might want to take account of this theory.[2]

Here's another example: Searching for "drug abuse" from 1996 to the present yielded 4,552 articles. Searching for "drug abuse" *and* "theory" yielded a more manageable 162 articles. Restricting the search by specifying that "theory" must appear in the *titles* of the articles,

---

[1] Swendsen, J. D. (1998). The helplessness-hopelessness theory and daily mood experience: An idiographic and cross-situational perspective. *Journal of Personality and Social Psychology, 74*, 1398–1408.

[2] Bushman, B. J. & Stack, A. D. (1996). Forbidden fruit versus tainted fruit: Effects of warning labels on attraction to television violence. *Journal of Experimental Psychology: Applied, 2*, 207–226.

identified an even more manageable 32 articles. Note that the word "theory" in the title of an article suggests that the article emphasizes one or more underlying theories in the conceptualization of the research. These would be good articles to examine if a researcher wants to relate his or her research to current theories.

Exercise for Topic 10

Directions: Consider the problem area that you believe you are most likely to pursue in your proposal.

1. In what problem area are you planning to conduct research?

2. Are you aware of any theories that might help you in planning your research?

3. Have you conducted an electronic database search using the term "theory?" If yes, what were the results? How helpful were the articles you identified by doing this?

Topic 11

Determining Feasibility

At this point, you should consider making a final selection of a problem area within which to propose research. You should also have a list of variables of interest within the area. The variables should have been derived from your study of research articles, including those with strong theoretical underpinnings. Also, you should combine variables into research questions. You should try to write a number of combinations so that you can evaluate them and choose the best among them.

For example, suppose that your broad problem area is homelessness and, more specifically, the origins of homelessness. Some of the variables you might consider are drug abuse, mental retardation, child abuse, strength of family ties, and so on. Some research questions you might ask are:

- Do homeless adults tend to have a stronger history of drug abuse than comparable people who are not homeless?

- Are the children of homeless parents more likely to become homeless adults than are children of housed parents?

- To what factors do the "new" homeless (i.e., those who have been homeless less than a year) attribute their homelessness?

As you know from Topic 4, you can rephrase a research *question* as a research *purpose* such as:

- The purpose is to identify the factors to which the "new" homeless attribute their homelessness.

Whether you use a *question* or a *purpose* is largely a matter of personal preference. However, if you think that you know the answer to a research question (i.e., you believe you can predict the answer), you should state a research *hypothesis* such as:

- It is hypothesized that children of homeless parents are more likely to become homeless adults than are children of housed parents.

Your next step is to take your list of possible questions, purposes, or hypotheses to experts (such as professors who have conducted research) for feedback. Of course, you will want to ask them to help you assess the importance of each in terms of making a contribution to your discipline. In addition, you should ask them to consider the *feasibility* of conducting research on each one. Having conducted research, they are in a better position than you (if you are a first-time researcher) to assess whether one question, purpose, or hypothesis will be inherently more difficult to gather data on than the others. This is important information if you will be conducting research with limited resources. For instance, for the examples in this topic, homeless participants will need to be contacted in person (since they cannot be mailed questionnaires). Do you have the resources (and inclination) to personally contact them? If you want to study the "new" homeless, how will you locate them? Will you be able to find a sufficient number of them? Are the homeless likely to be willing to participate in the type of study you are planning? These are examples of *feasibility* questions that would need to be answered before making a final selection.

Having selected research questions, purposes, or hypotheses that are both important and feasible, your next task is to select the appropriate research approach, a topic we will consider in the next section of this book.

Exercise for Topic 11

1. Write the name of your problem area here.

2. Write the research question(s), purpose(s), or hypothesis(es) on which your research will be based. (Keep in mind that you may wish to have a *set* of closely related ones that will be investigated in a single study. See the example at the end of Topic 7 and the example in the second column of Topic 13.)

3. Get feedback on the importance and feasibility of conducting the research suggested by your research questions, purposes, or hypotheses. Briefly describe your reactions to the feedback? Did it help you make a final selection?

Part C

Selecting an Approach

At this point, you should have selected a problem area and formulated research questions, purposes, or hypotheses on which to base your proposal.

In this part of the book, some important approaches to research (often called *types of research*) will be briefly summarized.[1] Since it is assumed that you have already taken a research methods course (or are taking one concurrently), the topics in this section of the book are designed to be only reminders of the major approaches and their characteristics. Logically, the selection of an approach should be driven by the nature of the research questions, purposes, or hypotheses. However, the entire process of planning research is interactive. For example, a research purpose might logically lead to a proposal to conduct *qualitative* research; yet, the potential researcher may not have training in how to conduct this type of research—leading to the need to revise or even abandon the initial research purpose in favor of a different one.

---

[1] Methods of research are classified in various ways by different authors of research methods textbooks. The ones reviewed in this section are the major ones commonly covered in most textbooks.

Notes

Topic 12

Qualitative Research

The purpose of qualitative research is to gain an *in-depth understanding of purposively selected participants from their perspective.*

The fact that it is *in-depth* rules out the use of typical questionnaires, tests, and psychological scales. Instead, qualitative researchers use techniques such as in-depth semi-structured interviews or direct observations over an extended period of time. In fact, sometimes qualitative researchers live with (such as living with a tribe) and work with (such as helping teachers conduct lessons) their participants. The resulting data does not lend itself to easy quantification, so qualitative researchers tend to report on themes and trends using words instead of statistics.

The use of *purposively selected participants* requires the researcher to have access to particular types of participants who are especially likely to help in gaining an understanding of a phenomenon. For example, if a research purpose is to understand the motivations of highly achieving African American women in the corporate world, the researcher would need to have access to and deliberately select such women.

Trying to understand participants *from their perspective* requires the researcher to bring an open mind to the research setting. Thus, *hypotheses* are usually an inappropriate basis for qualitative research. (Remember that a hypothesis is a prediction of a particular outcome, which implies prejudgment.) Rather, qualitative research typically rests on broad research *purposes* (or questions) such as:

- The purpose is to explore the intrinsic and extrinsic motivational factors to which highly achieving African American women attribute their success in the corporate world.

Because it is *from the participants' perspective*, qualitative researchers often ask their participants for feedback on their research findings (such as having them read the preliminary research report) and use this feedback in revising their interpretations of the findings.

Qualitative research is often recommended for new areas of research or areas about which social and behavioral scientists have little previous knowledge. (Note that it is difficult to draw up highly structured instruments such as a multiple-choice questionnaire to conduct quantitative research in a new area.) However, qualitative research is also desirable even in well-researched areas whenever in-depth information is needed.

Novice students who have limited knowledge of statistics may be drawn to qualitative research simply because statistics are not required in this type of research. With a little reflection, one can see that this is not a good reason for conducting qualitative research. It is relatively easy to find someone to help in the quantitative analysis and interpretation of scores obtained with objective measures. Getting expert help with sorting through hundreds of pages of transcribed material such as interview verbatims collected in qualitative research is a much more difficult matter. In other words, it is a myth that analyzing the results of qualitative research is inherently easier than analyzing the data collected in quantitative research.

Instead, qualitative research should be selected as the approach only if *in-depth* information about *particular types* of individuals is needed. In addition, potential researchers should be prepared to take one or more specialized courses to learn how to apply the diverse methods that constitute the qualitative approaches to research.

Exercise for Topic 12

1. Does your research purpose or question lend itself to qualitative research? Explain.

2. At this point, are you planning to propose qualitative research? If yes, will you be able to justify its selection for reasons other than merely a personal distaste for statistics? Explain.

3. If you are planning qualitative research, what type(s) of purposively selected participants do you anticipate using?

Topic 13

Survey Research

The purpose of a typical survey is to *collect information from a sample and generalize it to a larger population.* Political polls are a prime example in which only about 1,500 potential voters are questioned in order to estimate how all potential voters feel about candidates or issues.

The desire to *generalize* requires that an adequate sample be drawn such as a random sample (e.g., drawing names out of a hat) or stratified random sample (e.g., drawing names out of several hats with particular types of people such as "men" and "women" in different hats). In institutional settings, it is often possible for researchers with limited resources to get such samples. For example, with administrative approval, a teacher may be able to survey a random sample of students in his or her school in order to generalize to all students in the school.

Researchers interested in noninstitutionalized populations often conduct their surveys by mailing questionnaires. Many of these surveys have notoriously low rates of return (even with follow-up mailings), leaving researchers with information on only those who had sufficient time and interest to respond. If you conduct a survey by mail, you need to be prepared to warn your readers that the results are highly tentative and open to reinterpretation when surveys with better samples are conducted.

Typically, telephone surveys get a better response rate than mailed ones, and surveys conducted with in-person interviews do even better than telephone surveys.

Here is an example of a set of research hypotheses that lend themselves to survey research:

- It is hypothesized that the following groups of parents will be more in favor of mandatory uniforms in public schools:
  - (a) parents with children attending academically troubled schools (as opposed to those with children in high-achieving schools),
  - (b) parents with children in schools where there are patterns of student conflict and violence (as opposed to those with children in more peaceful schools), and
  - (c) parents whose economic resources are limited (as opposed to wealthier parents).

Notice that these hypotheses require that different groups of parents be compared with each other. For example, the attitudes of wealthier parents toward uniforms will need to be compared with the attitudes of poorer parents. Usually surveys in which comparisons are made are more interesting than surveys that just ask a single global question such as "What percentage of parents favor mandatory school uniforms for students in public school?"

Exercise for Topic 13

1. Does your research purpose or question lend itself to survey research? Explain.

2. At this point, are you planning to propose survey research? If yes, will you propose comparing two or more groups?

3. If you are planning survey research, how will you contact the participants (mail, telephone, in person, or electronically such as the Internet)?

4. If you have a low response rate, are you willing to advise your readers that your results should be viewed with considerable caution? Explain.

Topic 14

Correlational Research

In a simple correlational study, *two quantitative variables are measured* and the degree of relationship between them is determined by *computing a correlation coefficient*.

Most educational and psychological tests and scales yield quantitative scores[1] that could be used in correlational research. The following hypotheses lend themselves to correlational research.

- It is hypothesized that there is a *direct* correlation between College Board SAT scores and freshman GPA.

- It is hypothesized that depression and achievement motivation are *inversely* related.

A *direct* relationship is one in which those participants with high scores on one variable tend to have high scores on the other variable (and those with low scores on one variable have low scores on the other). For direct relationships, correlation coefficients range from 0.00 (no relationship) to 1.00 (perfect, direct relationship). It follows that values near 1.00 (such as .75 and above) are often called "very strong," and positive values near 0.00 (such as .25 and below) are often called "very weak."

An *inverse* relationship is one in which those participants who score high on one variable (such as being high in depression) score low on the other (such

as being low on achievement motivation). Values near –1.00 indicate a very strong inverse relationship, while negative values near 0.00 indicate a very weak one.

The two major reasons for conducting correlational research are (1) to estimate the validity of a test (such as the validity of the College Board's Scholastic Aptitude Test for predicting freshman GPA) and (2) to gain insights into interrelationships among variables (such as the relationship between depression and achievement motivation) in order to build and test theories.

It is important to note that correlation does not imply causality. For example, even if a strong inverse correlation were found between depression and achievement motivation, it is not clear whether high depression caused the low achievement motivation or something else caused the two to covary together (e.g., a hormonal imbalance might increase depression and decrease motivation *or* a learning disability might cause low achievement, which might reduce the motivation to strive to achieve as well as cause depression).

While a simple correlational study is confined to looking at two pairs of variables at a time, advanced correlational techniques allow researchers to look at variables in combination. For example, we could use a technique called *multiple regression* to determine how well high school grades when combined

---

[1] They should be quantitative and at the interval or ratio levels of measurement.

with College Board SAT scores predict freshman grades. It would be reasonable to hypothesize that the two predictors *in* *combination* will be a better predictor than either one individually.

Exercise for Topic 14

1. Does your research question, purpose, or hypothesis lend itself to correlational research? Explain.

2. At this point, are you planning to propose correlational research? If yes, will it be "simple" correlational research in which pairs of variables are correlated? (Note that more than one pair might be correlated in a given study.) If yes, name the pair(s) of variables that will be correlated.

3. If you are planning correlational research, will you be correlating some combination of variables (such as high school grades and SAT scores) with one *outcome* variable (such as freshman grades in college)? If yes, name the variables you will combine, and name the outcome variable.

Topic 15

Experimental Research

In Topic 5, you learned that the purpose of an experiment is to observe the effects of treatments on participants. A set of treatments (such as increasing the number of counselors in some high schools while not increasing them in others) constitutes the *independent variable*. The outcome (such as the number of violent acts per 100 students reported to the principal's office) is the *dependent variable*. Experiments usually are based on hypotheses (as opposed to research questions or purposes) since one would not ordinarily give treatments without expecting some type of response to them. This is a hypothesis that would naturally lead to an experiment:

- It is hypothesized that schools in which the number of school counselors is doubled will have fewer reports of violent acts than schools with the existing number of counselors.

When conducting experiments, it is desirable to assign participants at random (such as drawing names out of a hat) to conditions. For the hypothesis we are considering, ideally the students should be assigned at random to the schools and then schools should be assigned at random to either have the existing number of counselors or the increased number of counselors. The use of randomization to make assignments to treatment creates what is known as a *true experiment*.

When it is not possible to assign at random, useful experiments may still be conducted provided that great care is used in their execution. For example, perhaps a school board has decided to double the number of counselors in all schools in a district. To study the effects of this policy on school violence, a researcher might compare the incidence of violent acts in the school district before and after the additional counselors were hired. However, because school violence may be affected by larger forces in society outside of school, it would be highly desirable to compare the rates of violence in these schools with the rates in *comparable* schools in another district. The two sets of schools should be comparable in terms of preexisting rates of violence and other important demographics (such as family socioeconomic status, school funding, and so on). To the extent that the researcher can show comparability, the results will give a valid indication of the effects of increasing the number of counselors.

Interesting experiments can be conducted by examining two or more independent variables at the same time. For example, we might establish four groups of schools as follows:

	Increased number of counselors	Regular number of counselors
School uniforms	Group A	Group B
No school uniforms	Group C	Group D

This would allow a researcher to examine two issues simultaneously.

Exercise for Topic 15

1. Does your research hypothesis suggest an experiment? If yes, state your hypothesis. (Note: You may have two or more closely related hypotheses for a given study.)

2. If you will be conducting an experiment, do you anticipate assigning the participants at random to treatment conditions (i.e., conducting a true experiment)?

3. If you will be conducting an experiment and do *not* anticipate assigning the participants at random to treatment conditions, will you compare the experimental group with a *comparable* control group? If yes, on what types of variables do you plan to seek comparability?

Topic 16
Causal-Comparative Research

In the previous topic, you learned how cause-and-effect relationships might be examined by conducting an experiment. Sometimes, we are interested in identifying a cause *after* the effect or outcome has already been observed. For instance, we might observe that a large number of students dropped out of a local high school last year. Note that dropping out is an outcome or *dependent variable*. Research might be conducted to try to establish the cause (the *independent variable*). This would require *causal-comparative* research in which we look for the cause of some observation by looking to the past and comparing groups.

For example, we might have the following research purpose:

- The purpose is to explore the reasons for dropping out by interviewing dropouts with attention to school related variables such as the availability of counseling, perceptions of teachers' helpfulness, and other support services. As a point of comparison, nondropouts who are comparable on major sociodemographic variables will also be interviewed and their responses compared with those who dropped out.

A major danger in causal-comparative research is that an apparent cause may be coincidental to the true cause or even the result of the true cause. This is illustrated by this simplified example:

Example

Many employees who attended a large company picnic became ill with severe gastrointestinal distress. As a point of comparison, researchers contacted those who attended the picnic (a comparable group) but did not get ill. They found that those who got ill ate a green salad while those who did not get ill had not eaten the salad. At this point, the salad seems to be the culprit (cause). However, if they had stopped at this point, they would not have found the true cause. As it turns out, raw chicken was cut up for the picnic on the same unwashed cutting boards as the salads. Salmonella associated with the chicken—and not the salad *per se*—was the cause.

As a general rule, causal-comparative research should be undertaken only if an experiment cannot be conducted since researchers have more control over the participants' environment when conducting an experiment than when conducting a causal-comparative study. This extra measure of control allows those conducting experiments to rule out many alternative explanations for their results. However, for ethical and legal reasons, there are many types of treatments that cannot be given and must be studied after the fact. Here are a few examples of causal research questions that are not amenable to experimentation since we would not want to deliberately subject participants to the treatments implied by them:

- Is having physically abusive fathers a contributing factor to the development of abusiveness in young males?

- Do children who view violent media at a very early age tend to be more violent as teenagers than those who do not view it?
- Does incarceration of first-time offenders with dangerous prisoners guilty of serious offenses increase the odds that the first-time offenders will become hardened criminals?

In none of these cases would we want to deliberately subject participants to the implied treatments (such as showing violent media to very young children). Instead, we will need to work backwards with the causal-comparative method. For example, we might identify a group of violent teenagers and a group of nonviolent teenagers who are comparable in terms of demographics such as income, ethnicity, and so on. Comparing the amount of media violence each group was exposed to when they were young would give us some tentative answers to the research question.

Exercise for Topic 16

1. Does your research hypothesis suggest a causal-comparative study? Explain.

2. If you answered yes to question 1, what is your reason for conducting a causal-comparative study instead of an experiment?

3. If you answered yes to question 1, do you anticipate any difficulties in interpreting the results that you would not have if you had conducted an experiment? Explain.

Part D

Organizing and Evaluating Literature

At this point, you should have selected a problem area and formulated research questions, purposes, or hypotheses on which to base your proposal. In addition, you should have selected a research approach. Finally, you should have conducted an extensive search of the literature with an emphasis on locating research articles published in academic journals.

A typical research proposal begins with an introduction that relies heavily on the research literature on your topic. Before beginning to write, you should review, evaluate, and organize the literature you have collected. These tasks are covered in this part of the book.

Notes

Topic 17

Organizing Literature by Topics

Begin by sorting the research articles you have collected according to the topic(s) they cover. Because many research articles may cover more than one topic you wish to review, this task is a bit more difficult than you might anticipate at first. Here is a way to simplify the task:

A. Give each article a number. It does not matter what number you give each article as long as each one has a different number.

B. As you read the articles, begin preparing a tentative list of various subtopics that you might cover in your literature review. Revise this as you proceed through the literature. Get feedback on this list.

C. Prepare a set of 3-by-5 note cards on which you write the name of a single subtopic. On the card, write the article number(s) that contain information on the topic. Note that one article may cover more than one topic.

Consider this simple example. Suppose your research hypothesis is that small cooperative learning groups in college algebra classes will improve student achievement, persistence, and attitudes toward math. Here are some of the *topics* that might be written on a card:[1]

---

[1] The topics for this example were drawn from Springer, L., Stanne, M. E., & Donovan, S. S. (1999). Effects of small-group learning on undergraduates in science, mathematics, engineering, and technology: A meta-analysis. *Review of Educational Research, 69,* 21–51.

Topics

1. Need for improvement in college math instruction (in general).
2. Definitions of cooperative learning.
3. Arguments favoring cooperative learning (including theories of instruction and learning that support it).
4. Extent to which cooperative learning is currently being used in college-level classrooms.
5. Achievement as an outcome of cooperative learning.
6. Persistence as an outcome of cooperative learning.
7. Attitudes toward math as an outcome of cooperative learning.

Suppose that the article you numbered as #1 contains an especially good definition of cooperative learning and also reports on an experiment in which student achievement was examined. You should write "#1" on the cards for definitions (Topic 2) and achievement (Topic 5).

If you are dealing with an especially large body of literature, you may wish to develop subcategories under the major topics. For example, Topic 5 might have two cards: one for studies that show improvement in achievement as a result of cooperative learning and one for those that fail to show an improvement in achievement.

Depending on the nature of the literature you are reviewing, you might want to have a separate card for each type of research (see Part C of this book). For example, you might have a card for qualitative research, one for survey research, and so on. You might also wish to have a card for various types of participants in the research. For instance, there might be one card for *high school* (studies of cooperative learning with high school students) and *college* (studies with college students). Note that those with college students are more relevant to the hypothesis we are considering, but the literature on high-school students might contain important information you wish to review.

The system suggested here will prepare you to organize your literature review *by topics*. In other words, it will help you write one that moves from topic to topic with appropriate citations to the literature. Note that a given article may be cited in one *or more* topic discussions at various points in a literature review.

Exercise for Topic 17

1. List some major topics that relate to each of your research questions, purposes, or hypotheses. (This should be based on your initial reading of the literature.)

2. As you read the literature again, consider whether you should add additional topics or subtopics. If so, list them here.

3. Number the articles you have collected, and prepare a set of topic cards as described above. Write your reactions to the process here. Did you find some things hard to classify? Did you get a better understanding of your literature as a result of following the recommendations in this topic? Explain.

Topic 18
Evaluating Research Literature

In preparation for writing the introduction and literature review for your proposal, you should evaluate the empirical studies you located in your literature search. This is important because, other things being equal, you will want to emphasize the stronger studies while warning your readers about extremely weak studies that you cite.[1]

Since it is assumed that you have taken a research methods course in which you learned how to distinguish strong studies from weak ones, this topic is designed to be a refresher on three of the most salient issues in evaluating research.

First is the issue of *sampling*. *Quantitative researchers* emphasize the use of solid sampling techniques such as simple random or stratified random sampling so that the results of the study can be generalized with confidence to the population from which the sample was drawn. However, many researchers lack the resources or cooperation from participants to obtain such samples, so you will need to decide which studies have better samples. Often, this will be clear such as when one researcher has a high rate of response to a mailed survey while another one has a low rate.

When evaluating samples, also consider the diversity of the samples (even if they are biased). For example, a study on communication pattern differences be-

tween husbands and wives that is based only on married college students is less diverse than a sample consisting of college students *and* members of the broader community that might be solicited through classified advertisements and contacts with community agencies, churches, and so on.

You should also consider how closely the samples used in the literature correspond to the samples you will be using. For example, if you will be studying college students enrolled in a college-level mathematics class, research based on middle-school students in mathematics may be a tenuous match.

When evaluating the samples used by *qualitative researchers*, ask if the samples are truly purposive (see Topic 12) or are merely convenience samples (people who happened to be convenient to the researchers).

The second issue is *measurement*. Do the researchers provide you with information on the reliability and validity of their measurement techniques, keeping in mind that none should be presumed to be perfect? Do the measures seem suitable for the research purposes? Have the researchers used multiple methods/ sources to measure crucial variables? For example, a study on designated driving that relies solely on self-reports by participants is less strong than one that supplements self-reports with direct observations of behavior. Multiple sources of

---

[1] Methods for critiquing weak studies are discussed in Topic 24.

43

information can also be obtained by asking a variety of sources to report on the same phenomenon. For example, a study in which students' self-report on their academic motivation would be stronger if teachers and parents are also asked to report on the same students' motivation.

The third issue is *conclusions*. Check to determine the extent to which the conclusions reached by the researchers are substantiated by the research. You will not want to cite strongly stated conclusions based on weak studies without warning your readers.

Exercise for Topic 18

1. Select one of the research articles that you identified in your literature search.

    A. Briefly evaluate the sample:

    B. Briefly evaluate the measurement procedures:

    C. Briefly evaluate the conclusions in light of the research methodology:

2. Select another one of the research articles that you identified in your literature search.

    A. Briefly evaluate the sample:

    B. Briefly evaluate the measurement procedures:

    C. Briefly evaluate the conclusions in light of the research methodology:

Topic 19

Considering the History of a Topic

In your literature review, you may want to provide a historical perspective to help establish the context in which you will be conducting research. This is especially true if you are writing a proposal for a thesis or dissertation because your committee may want to be sure that you know *where you are coming from* as well as *where you hope to go.*

To gain a historical perspective, put the research articles you have collected in chronological order from oldest to newest. Then examine them to look for changes over time. Be especially careful to notice changes of the following types:

- *Changes in definitions.* For example, have definitions of physical child abuse changed to include milder forms of abuse (such as spanking) over time? If so, this may account for the increased reporting of child abuse cases. You will need to decide whether to use the newer or older definition(s) and inform your readers of the basis for your decision.

- *New terminology.* For example, there is a long history of studies of *burnout* and stress among psychotherapists. However, a newer term such as *vicarious traumatization* (psychotherapists becoming fundamentally traumatized through their empathy with traumatized clients) may signal a new line of thought and research on this topic.[1] You may wish to point out how research on *burnout* differs from research based on the newer term.

- *Changes in theoretical underpinnings.* For example, do the authors of older research trace its origins to Freud while newer research emphasizes Ellis's theory? If so, you will want to point this out to your readers.

In addition, you should look for *key players*—those who have built a research career conducting research on your topic. These are easy to spot because they will have authored or coauthored a number of articles on the topic and will be frequently cited by others who have conducted the research you have collected. If you find that there is one essential key player, you may wish to briefly trace how this person has contributed to and moved the research in your problem area forward when you write your literature review.

In your quest for a historical overview on your topic, you may find assistance in the writings of others. Other researchers sometimes provide a historical overview in the introductions to their research articles, which you might use as the starting point for writing your own overview.

---

[1] For more information on this topic, consult Brady, J. L., Guy, J. E., Poelstra, P. L., & Brokaw, B. F. (1999). Vicarious traumatization, spirituality, and the treatment of sexual abuse survivors: A national survey of women psychotherapists. *Professional Psychology: Research and Practice, 30,* 386–393.

Exercise for Topic 19

1. Put the research articles you have collected into chronological order and examine them. Have the definitions of key terms in your area changed over time? Explain.

2. Has new terminology been introduced? Explain.

3. Have there been changes in the theoretical underpinnings in the area you will be studying? Explain.

4. Is there a key player? Do you think it will be worthwhile to trace his or her historical contributions to your area of research? Explain.

Part E

Writing the Introduction and Literature Review

Having worked through Parts A through D of this book, you are now ready to begin writing. Before beginning, determine whether the introduction needs to be separate from the literature review or whether the literature review should be integrated with the introductory remarks. The sample proposals near the end of this book illustrate the latter.

Topic 20 in this part of the book provides suggestions for those who will be writing a separate introduction, which is often required of thesis and dissertation students. Topic 21 deals with the integration of an introduction with a literature review. The remaining topics deal with the development of an effective literature review.

The following outline shows the components of a typical research proposal. We will refer to this outline at the beginning of each of the remaining parts of this book to help you get the big picture of where you are and where you will be going while writing your proposal.

I.	Introduction	←*You are here.*
II.	Literature Review*	←*You are here.*
III.	Method	
	A. Participants	
	B. Instrumentation	
	C. Procedures	
IV.	Analysis	
V.	Discussion**	

*May be integrated with the Introduction.
**Followed by writing a title and an abstract as well as developing a timeline.

Notes

Topic 20

A Separate Introduction

If your thesis/dissertation committee, instructor, or potential funding agency requires a separate introduction to the research proposal (that is, separate from the literature review), try to determine whether there are guidelines on what is to be covered by it. If there are specific guidelines, follow them carefully. The following suggestions are for those who are required to write a separate introduction but do not have specific guidelines. Note that some of these suggestions will be explored again in more detail in later topics.

- Your first paragraph should introduce the *specific* problem area in which you will be conducting research. If your problem area is the effects of rewards on creative behavior in the classroom, do *not* start with a discussion of the importance of education in a technological society. Instead, start by discussing why educators are interested in fostering creativity.

- As soon as possible, establish that your problem area is important. This can be done in a number of ways. For example, you might be able to point out that government agencies or prominent scholars have called for additional research in your area. You might also have some statistics on how many people are affected by the problem you are proposing to investigate.

- Provide definitions of key terms. For example, how is "creativity" defined by other scholars? What is your definition?

- Provide an overview of the important points and trends in the literature you have read. Do not get too specific. For example, you might say, "As the literature review that follows shows, several experiments suggest that creativity is not enhanced by the provision of material rewards. This finding is consistent with the theory of...." (In the literature review, of course, you will want to cite the specific experiments and provide some details on them.)

- Provide an overview of your proposed research methodology. What *type* of research are you proposing (e.g., qualitative, survey, and so on)? Why did you select that type?

- Point out why *your particular study* is needed. For instance, given that a number of studies on the effects of rewards on creativity have already been conducted, how will your study advance knowledge in this area? Will you use a better sample? Will you examine a different type of creativity? These issues usually should be addressed in general terms; the specifics will be addressed later in the proposal when you present your proposed methodology.

49

- Discuss in general terms the broad implications of your proposed research. Note that a detailed discussion will be provided in the last section of your proposal.

By following these suggestions, your introduction will provide a broad overview of your proposal, which will help your readers by showing them the big picture before they begin reading for details in the subsequent sections of the proposal. Many students may find that it is easier to write the introduction after writing the body of the proposal on which the introduction is based.

Exercise for Topic 20

1. Determine whether you are required to write an introduction that is separate from the literature review. If you are, what guidelines, if any, exist for this activity?

2. Prepare a topic outline of what you will cover in your introduction. Refer to any guidelines that you have been given as well as to the suggestions in this topic.

3. Get feedback from instructors and colleagues on the topic outline you have written. Revise it in light of their suggestions.

4. Will you write your separate introduction now, or will you wait until after you have completed the rest of the proposal? Explain.

Topic 21

An Integrated Introduction and Literature Review

The previous topic provides guidelines for writing a separate introduction. If you will be writing an introduction integrated with your literature review, you will be covering the same territory, but will be relying heavily on specifics from the literature to support your points.

As in the case of a separate introduction, the first paragraph should introduce the *specific* problem area—not some broad general topic. Also use the first paragraph or two to establish the importance of your research problem, using specifics from the literature to support your contention. Arguably, the first paragraph of a proposal is the most important since a strong beginning is likely to convince readers that the remainder of the proposal is worthy of careful consideration. It is so important that the next topic in this book is devoted to writing the first paragraph.

In an integrated introduction and literature review, key terms should be defined early. Usually, conceptual (dictionary-like) definitions are sufficient. Operational definitions that describe how you identified or measured the variables will be presented later in the proposal. The following example presents a conceptual definition. Note that it is not necessary to "create" new definitions if previously published ones are adequate.

Example

Social support is characterized by affective support (i.e., love, liking, and respect), confirmation (i.e., confirming the moral and actual "rightness" of actions and statements), and direct help (e.g., aid in work, giving information and money; Kahn & Antonucci, 1980).[1]

Following the definitions, literature should be cited that shows the development of intellectual thought on your issue and a discussion of the major findings. The following topics in this part of the book provide guidance on how to do this. At this point, however, note that an effective literature review presents the literature *from your point of view*. In other words, you are responsible for organizing the literature into related various topical groups and for showing your reader how it "fits together" (or fails to do so). To do this, you will need to add commentary and not simply write a string of summaries of individual studies.

As you write your review of literature, point out which studies are most closely allied with your proposed study. In addition, discuss how your study is similar to (as well as different from) those that were previously published.

---

[1] Frese, M. (1999). Social support as a moderator of the relationship between work stressors and psychological dysfunctioning: A longitudinal study with objective measures. *Journal of Occupational Health Psychology, 4,* 179–192.

Typically, a literature review (whether it is written as a separate section or is integrated with the introduction) ends with the specific research questions, purposes, or hypotheses that are the basis for your proposal. If your literature review is well constructed, your questions, purposes, or hypotheses will be seen by your readers as a natural outgrowth of the literature you have reviewed for them.

Note that if you are required to write a separate introduction (see Topic 20), you may be required to conclude it with a statement of the research questions, purposes, or hypotheses that you will be researching. If so, you may not want to repeat them at the end of the literature review.

Exercise for Topic 21

1. What key terms will you be defining at the conceptual level? Will you be creating new definitions or using those suggested by others? Explain.

2. Do you have a *point of view* on the literature you have read (e.g., Do you have a sense of what it means *as a whole*)? Explain.

3. Do you anticipate that you will be able to show your readers how your research questions, purposes, or hypotheses naturally flow from the literature you are reviewing? Explain.

Topic 22
Writing the First Paragraph(s)

The first paragraph of your proposal (whether it is a separate introduction or an integrated introduction and literature review) should identify the specific problem area. This paragraph normally should also be used to establish (or start to establish) its importance.

One technique for establishing the current need for a study in an area is to cite specific statistics showing that a particular population that is not well understood is increasing in numbers. This was done by the authors of Example 1.

Example 1

The number of temporary employees has increased from 20,000 in 1956 (Gannon, 1984) to 760,000 in 1986 (Pollock, 1986), 1.6 million in 1993 (Sunoo, 1994), and 2.3 million in 1996 (Neuborne, 1997). Temporary employees have been estimated to represent around 20% of the workforce (Caudron, 1994). Although the use of temporary employees has been rising, there has been limited research focused on this sample, including little investigation of....[1]

Note that the statement in Example 1 is much stronger than a nonstatistical general statement such as "The number of temporary employees has increased greatly in recent years."

Another way to establish the importance of a research problem is to show that the topic has been investigated over time, and findings with important impli-

cations have been obtained. This is done in Example 2.

Example 2

Interest in the role that social relationships play in promoting health and well-being has a long and rich history (Burgess, 1926; Park & Burgess, 1926). This interest has been fueled in recent decades by findings from prospective studies that link social network involvement to health outcomes (Berkman & Syme, 1979; House, Robbins, & Metzner, 1982). For example, in several epidemiological studies, socially isolated men were 2–4 times more likely than nonisolated men to die during follow-up periods of 9–11 years....[2]

Another technique is to cite the calls by prominent people or organizations for research in an area. Example 3 illustrates this.

Example 3

What students learn is greatly influenced by how they learn, and many students learn best through active, collaborative, small-group work inside and outside the classroom. The National Science Foundation (1996), for example, recommends that students have frequent access to active learning experiences in class and out of class (as through study groups).[3]

Whatever approach you take, be prepared to write and rewrite the first paragraph until you have a strong, demanding beginning. Get feedback from

---

[1] Chen, P. Y., Popovich, P. M., & Kogan, M. (1999). Let's talk: Patterns and correlates of social support among temporary employees. *Journal of Occupational Health Psychology, 4,* 55–62.

[2] Lewis, M. A. & Rook, K. S. (1999). Social control in personal relationships: Impact on health behaviors and psychological distress. *Health Psychology, 18,* 63–71.
[3] Springer, L., Stanne, M. E., & Donovan, S. S. (1999). Effects of small-group learning on undergraduates in science, mathematics, engineering, and technology: A meta-analysis. *Review of Educational Research, 69,* 21–51.

others, and carefully consider their assessments during this process.

Exercise for Topic 22

1. Will you be using one of the three techniques discussed in this topic in the first paragraph of your proposal? Explain.

2. From whom will you get feedback on your first paragraph?

Topic 23

Using a Topic Outline

Developing and following a topic outline while writing helps to produce focused, logical prose. When dealing with a large amount of literature, it will also help you avoid becoming overwhelmed by the volume of material to be covered.

You were urged to organize the literature you collected by topics in Topic 17, to put the name of each topic on a card, and to write the article numbers that touched on each topic on the cards. At this point, try sorting and resorting the cards to establish the order in which the topics will be addressed in your literature review. Then prepare a topic outline.

Here is a sample topic outline for a literature review:[1]

Problem area: Career Plans of Science-Talented
Rural Adolescent Girls

1. Name specific problem area
2. The gender gap in science (establish importance)
   a. Underrepresentation of women in the sciences
   b. Greater representation of women in the biological sciences than physical sciences
   c. Less positive attitudes toward science among female students
   d. Lack of previous studies on rural female students
3. Factors related to career decisions in science
   a. Influence of parents' beliefs
      (1) Expectations for their own children
      (2) Parents' sex-role stereotypes regarding science
   b. Influence of peers
      (1) Influence on achievement motivation
      (2) Influence on selection of science courses in high school
   c. Influence of extracurricular activities

   d. Influence of perceived intrinsic value of science
      (1) The expectancy-value model of achievement choices
      (2) Link between intrinsic value and achievement
      (3) Gender differences in valuing science (interest)
4. Statement of the research hypotheses

Next, you should begin writing while referring to your topic cards for appropriate references. Note that more than one reference may be used to substantiate a given point. In the following example, for instance, two studies are cited for the finding described in the first sentence.

Example

Some studies have found that peers have an indirect impact on career decision making by influencing the classes that students choose to take (Cohen & Cohen, 1980; Smail, 1985). Students report being more worried about what their friends will think than about whether they can handle the class work (Beal, 1994); they say that friends have a strong influence through their actions and their encouraging or discouraging comments, leading them to choose a class or career that a friend has chosen (Bender, 1994).[2]

If you are writing a long review (say three or more pages), it is very desirable to use major headings and subheadings within the review. The topics in your topic outline can be used as such subheadings. For example, point 3 (Factors related to career decisions in science) could be a major heading and 3a (Influence of parents' beliefs), 3b, 3c, and 3d could be subheadings.

---

[1] This topic outline is loosely based on the work of Jacobs, J. E., Finken, L. L., Griffin, N. L., & Wright, J. D. (1998). The career plans of science-talented rural adolescent girls. *American Educational Research Journal, 35,* 681–704.

[2] Ibid.

For a long literature review, you should consider writing a summary of the review, pointing out the highlights of the material you covered. Usually, this should be placed just before the statement of research purposes, questions, or hypotheses that conclude the review.

Exercise for Topic 23

1. Write a topic outline on which to base your literature review.

2. Do you anticipate using major headings/subheadings within your review? Explain.

3. Did you remember to end your outline with the research questions, purposes, or hypotheses? If you have decided not to place them at the end, where will they be placed?

Topic 24

Being Selective and Critical

The literature covered in a typical research proposal should be selective. Generally, you should select those articles that bear most directly on your research plans. If there are many of this type, select and emphasize those that have the strongest research methodology (see Topic 18 for reminders on evaluating research literature). Other things being equal, more recent research should be emphasized over older research except when providing a historical overview on your research topic (see Topic 19 on providing a historical overview).

If you will be citing just some of the studies that support a statement, use "e.g.," meaning "for example," as is done in Example 1.

Example 1

In support of such assumptions is research showing that adult children of alcoholics (ACAs) are more prone to psychological and physical distress than are adult children of nonalcoholics (non-ACAs; e.g., Black, Bucky, & Wilder-Padilla, 1986; Kashubeck, 1994; Taliaferro & Aponte, 1990). For example, researchers have reported that ACAs are at greater risk than non-ACAs for problems with low self-esteem, anxiety, and depression (e.g., Domenico & Windle, 1993).[1]

Note that if you are writing a research proposal for a thesis or disserta-

tion, your committee may expect you to be comprehensive in your citations to demonstrate that you are familiar with all the literature with a direct bearing on your proposal. Thus, you may not be permitted to use the technique of citing just examples of studies that support a certain point.

In addition to being selective, you should also be critical. You can warn your readers of tenuous results with various techniques such as referring to a weak study as a pilot study or by referring to certain specific weaknesses such as having a very small sample. Example 2 illustrates these techniques.

Example 2

In a series of pilot studies, X was found to precede Y in most cases (Smith, 2000).

Based on interviews with five teenage boys, Jones (1999) found that A is stronger than B.

You should also consider critiquing groups of studies on a given topic if they all have a common weakness (or strength). Example 3 illustrates this.

Example 3

Many of the studies comparing ACAs and non-ACAs failed to control for the presence of other types of family dysfunction besides parental alcoholism in the non-ACA group. Certainly, the experience of other family problems such as parental psychiatric illness, domestic violence, incest, and chronic illness might affect the family's ability to meet the physical and emotional needs of the children.

You should also point out gaps in the literature. Are there unstudied groups

---

[1] Examples 1 and 3 are based on the work of Robitschek, C. & Kashubeck, S. (1999). A structural model of parent alcoholism, family functioning, and psychological health: The mediating effects of hardiness and personal growth orientation. *Journal of Counseling Psychology, 46*, 159–172.

and variables? Have researchers tackled your problem only from one theoretical perspective and not others? A strong feature of any proposal is being able to show that the proposed study will help fill in a gap in our knowledge of an important topic.

Exercise for Topic 24

1. How selective will you be when you write your literature review? Explain.

2. Do you have sufficient command of the literature that you have collected to be critical? Are there groups of articles with a common weakness? Explain.

3. Are there gaps in the literature? Will your study fill in the gaps? Explain.

Part F

Proposing a Sample

In a typical research proposal, the introduction and literature review are followed by a description of the proposed research methodology. This section of the report is usually identified with the major heading "Method," followed by a subheading "Participants" or "Subjects." It is in this section that you should describe your proposed sample. Note "Participants" should be used if the individuals in your study are freely participating with knowledge of the purposes of the research. On the other hand, "Subjects" is more appropriate if the individuals do not know they are being studied or are coerced to be in a study.[1] Some researchers prefer to use the subheading "Respondents" when referring to individuals who have responded to a survey.

I.	Introduction	
II.	Literature Review*	
III.	Method	
	A. Participants	←*You are here.*
	B. Instrumentation	
	C. Procedures	
IV.	Analysis	
V.	Discussion**	

*May be integrated with the Introduction.
**Followed by writing a title and an abstract as well as developing a timeline.

---

[1] For ethical and legal reasons, most researchers avoid coercion to obtain a sample. However, there are many examples of subjects being observed in public places without their knowledge that they are part of a study. For example, we might observe drivers' behavior in parking lots or teenagers' behavior in shopping malls.

Notes

Topic 25
Sampling in Qualitative Research

In Topic 12, you learned that the purpose of qualitative research is to gain an *in-depth understanding of purposively selected participants from their perspective.* Hence, if you will be conducting qualitative research, you should propose to purposively select participants who meet *criteria* that will yield a sample that is likely to provide the types of information you need to achieve your research purpose.

Consider an example. Suppose your research purpose is to explore the nature and extent of the psychological and social support new teachers receive from other teachers, school administrators, and other school personnel with attention to the relationship between such support and their satisfaction in their jobs as teachers. Obviously, one *criterion* you will use is that the teacher-participants will need to be new teachers. Other criteria you might consider are: (1) Will you restrict the sample to fully trained and credentialed (i.e., licensed) teachers, or will you include teachers who are teaching on an emergency credential (not fully trained and licensed)? (2) Will you include teachers who teach in urban, suburban, and rural areas, or will you restrict the sample to those in just one type of area? (3) Will you include both male and female teachers? (4) Will you include elementary, middle-school, and high school teachers or restrict it to just one type? After thinking through such questions,

you should prepare a statement of the criteria for selection of participants to include in your proposal. Here is an example of such a statement:

Example
Criteria for participant selection will be as follows. The teacher-participants must be fully credentialed and in their first or second year of teaching at the elementary level in a large urban school district. They will be selected without regard to gender. However, it is anticipated that there will be more females than males in the sample because the teaching profession at the elementary level is female-dominated.

Next, you should propose a method for locating participants who meet your selection criteria. Will you telephone elementary-school principals throughout an urban school district and request their cooperation in identifying teachers who meet your criteria? Will you use just the three teachers who meet these criteria at your neighborhood elementary school where you are already on friendly terms with the principal? Either of these possibilities is acceptable, but note that the second one will limit your study to teachers in one particular school. Will those who will be evaluating your proposal find this acceptable? Is there something special about this school (e.g., a school with a reputation for high academic achievement) that makes it especially interesting? If so, you should address this issue in your proposal.

Note that sample size usually is not a major issue in qualitative research.

Since you will be striving for in-depth information, you will probably not be expected to use a large number of participants. It is more important to spend enough time with a small number than to work superficially with a large number.

Note that qualitative researchers sometimes start with a small number of participants and continue adding more until they reach the point of redundancy (i.e., when they find that the newly added participants are not contributing information or insights beyond those already obtained with previous participants). However, in your proposal, you should consider stating an anticipated number of participants or a ballpark number that would be the maximum you believe you could work with during your time frame and within your resources. This is especially true of thesis and dissertation students who will want feedback from their committees regarding their proposed sample.

Exercise for Topic 25

1. If you are proposing qualitative research, write your research purpose or question here.

2. Write a statement that names the criteria you propose to use in selecting participants.

3. Write a statement that describes how you propose to locate participants who meet your criteria.

4. Do you have an anticipated sample size? Explain. Do you have a maximum number in mind with which you have the resources to work? Explain. Will you sample to the point of redundancy? Explain.

Topic 26

Random Sampling

In quantitative research, the ideal is to identify a population of interest and sample from it at random. Random sampling gives each person in the population an equal and independent chance of being selected. A sample drawn at random is, by definition, unbiased. Drawing names out of a hat is one way to obtain a random sample. Equivalent results can be obtained using a table of random numbers or computer generated random samples. Be careful to distinguish between *random sampling* and *accidental sampling* (also known as convenience sampling). Selecting individuals who happen to be available is *not* random sampling.

In order to give every individual an equal chance, you will need to know the identities of each one of them as well as how to contact them (e.g., an address). Often researchers have this knowledge for only a subset of the population of interest. This is called the *sampling frame*, that is, the set of individuals accessible to a researcher. For example, suppose your research purpose calls for contacting all students who have graduated from a school during the past ten years. You will probably find that the alumni records (with current addresses) are incomplete because the alumni office has lost contact with many of the graduates. Thus, your sample will need to be drawn from the subset for whom current addresses are available. The following example shows how this might be proposed.

Example

The population for this study consists of all graduates of Eisenhower High School from 1991 through 2000. However, the alumni office estimates that it has current addresses for only 71% ($n = 6,745$) of this population. These 6,745 graduates will constitute the sampling frame from which a simple random sample of 11% ($n = 742$) will be contacted by mail to participate in the study.

Notice the use of the term *simple random sample* in the example. The adjective "simple" refers to drawing the sample in one step from the entire sampling frame. In contrast, in a *stratified random sample*, the individuals in the sampling frame are divided into known subgroups, and a fixed percentage is drawn from each subgroup. For example, if we divide those in the sampling frame into males and females and draw 11% of the males and 11% of the females, we have stratified on the basis of gender, which results in a sample that is representative in terms of this characteristic. If you will be using stratified random sampling, you should indicate the basis for stratification (e.g., gender) in your proposal. The last sentence of the example could be rewritten as follows: "These 6,745 graduates will constitute the sampling frame from which a sample of 11% ($n = 742$) stratified on the basis of gender will be drawn."

Other methods of sampling as well as the issue of sample size are covered in subsequent topics in this part of the book.

Exercise for Topic 26

1. Do you know the identities and have contact information for the entire population of interest to you? If no, do you have this information on a sampling frame within the population? Explain.

2. Do you plan to draw a simple random sample for your study? If yes, write a first draft of a statement to that effect.

3. Do you plan to draw a stratified random sample for your study? If yes, write a first draft of a statement to that effect.

Topic 27
Other Methods of Sampling: I

Although random sampling is preferred in quantitative research (see Topic 26), quantitative researchers often do not have sufficient knowledge of a population or do not have the resources to obtain such a sample. In this topic, we will consider two other methods of sampling and how they might be proposed.

Suppose your research purpose is to explore safe-sex practices among injecting drug abusers who have not had contact with law enforcement and have not sought treatment for their addiction. Obviously, there is no master list of such individuals (with contact information) from which you could draw a random sample. However, if you could identify even a few such individuals (perhaps through people who are currently seeking treatment), these few could put you in touch with others who could then provide you with additional names so that your sample grows geometrically like a snowball. In fact, this type of sampling is known as *snowball sampling*. Example 1 shows how this might be proposed.

Example 1

To obtain a sample of injecting drug abusers who have not had contact with law enforcement and have not sought treatment, clients at a public and a private drug abuse treatment center will be asked to contact personal acquaintances who meet the criteria for participation in this study. Specifically, the directors of the two treatment centers have agreed to allow their social workers to distribute flyers to their clients. The flyers will briefly describe the purposes of the proposed research and will include information on how the researchers can be contacted by phone. The flyers will guarantee anonymity and will offer a token reward of $10.00 for participation in a half-hour interview. Those who respond to this offer will be asked to nominate additional potential participants. This snowball technique will be used until a sample of at least 24 participants is obtained.

For practical reasons, researchers sometimes plan to use samples that happen to be readily available to them. These are known as *convenience* or *accidental* samples. If you will be using such a sample, any generalizations from it to a population will have to be made with great caution. Usually, it is best to address this issue directly when describing your proposed sample as illustrated in Example 2.

Example 2

The participants in this study will be approximately 120 college freshmen and sophomores who are taking required introductory courses in the social and behavioral sciences at Doe University. Students are required to participate in a study of their choice from those listed by the department and receive course credit for their participation. Thus, the sample will not be randomly selected, which will limit the generalizability of the results. However, the fact that the courses are required for all students makes it likely that the sample will be diverse in terms of students' majors.

If you find you must propose using a sample of convenience, consider whether it will be possible to propose one that has *diversity*. For example, a proposal stating that students will be drawn from required courses at two or three colleges and universities (e.g., public, large private, and small liberal arts) will be stronger than one that relies on students at only one institution. Likewise, if a researcher is going to propose approaching students on campus to interview them, a sample obtained at various times of the day and at diverse locations on campus would be stronger than one in which only students entering the cafeteria at lunchtime would be sampled.

Note that for survey work in which the emphasis is on making sound generalizations to a population (such as a political poll of potential voters), proposing a convenience sample might doom the proposal. Convenience samples are more acceptable when researchers are conducting preliminary studies of a phenomenon or when gathering data for theory building in which the proposed convenience sample is only one of many different types of samples that will be studied in the long run.

Exercise for Topic 27

1. Do you plan to use snowball sampling? If yes, write a description of how you will sample.

2. Do you plan to use a sample of convenience? If yes, write a description of how you will sample.

Other Methods of Sampling: II

If you are planning to study a population that is divided into a number of naturally existing groups with leaders, you might consider using *cluster sampling*. For example, all students in a high school typically have a homeroom with a homeroom teacher (the leader). Rather than drawing individual names at random and then trying to contact individual students who will be scattered throughout the school, you might find it more convenient to draw a random sample of homerooms (i.e., clusters) and ask the homeroom teachers to gather the data for you (i.e., ask them to distribute questionnaires). Of course, you will want to draw a number of the homerooms. For instance, drawing only one homeroom with 30 students would not give you a good sample of 30 students if it happened to be a homeroom for the academically talented. Example 1 shows how cluster sampling might be proposed.

Example 1

Cluster sampling will be used to obtain the sample for this study. Specifically, 20% of the homerooms ($n = 25$) in each of the four high schools in the school district will be selected at random. With administrative approval, the homeroom teachers will be asked to distribute and collect the completed questionnaires during the first homeroom period of the semester. Since the average class size in the district is 22, approximately 550 students will participate in the survey.[1]

The use of cluster sampling is not limited to school settings. It can be used for sampling from any population that is already separated into groups such as Girl Scouts (who are in troops) and members of the Southern Baptist Convention (who are in congregations).

Multistage sampling is sometimes useful when sampling from a large population. For example, suppose you want to sample registered nurses employed by hospitals in California. To use simple random sampling, you would need to get the names and contact information for all such nurses in order to give them all an equal chance when sampling (e.g., all their names must be in the hat). An alternative is to obtain a master list of all licensed hospitals in California and proceed as illustrated in Example 2.

Example 2

Multistage, stratified random sampling will be used to obtain the sample for this study. Specifically, the hospitals on a master list of all licensed hospitals in California will be divided into three groups: rural, urban, and suburban hospitals. From each group, 30% of the hospitals will be randomly selected. Appropriate administrators at each of the selected hospitals will be contacted by telephone to solicit their cooperation in identifying a random sample of 20% of the nurses they employ....

In Topics 25 through 28, we have considered various types of sampling plans that might be proposed. Typically, *how* you sample (e.g., at random) will be more important than *how many* you sam-

---

[1] Note that *sample size* in this example is 25—not 550. For statistical reasons, the number of *units* selected at random determines the sample size.

ple when your proposal is evaluated. Nevertheless, you should propose sampling some specific number of participants—even if it is only a ballpark figure. Topic 29 deals with this issue.

Exercise for Topic 28

1. Do you plan to use cluster sampling? If yes, write a description of how you will sample.

2. Do you plan to use multistage sampling? If yes, write a description of how you will sample.

Sample Size

When novice researchers begin planning their research, one of the questions that they often ask is, "How large does my sample have to be?" Unfortunately, there are no simple answers. In this topic, we will explore some practical considerations that bear on sample size.

First, review the literature you have collected to determine the typical sample size used in studies that are similar to yours. Pay particular attention to studies that employ the same method of research that you are planning. For example, you will probably find that qualitative studies typically are based on much smaller samples than surveys.

Second, consider your resources. If you are a thesis or dissertation student with limited funds, even the cost of duplicating large numbers of questionnaires (let alone mailing costs) could be prohibitive if you propose studying a large sample. Likewise, conducting face-to-face interviews with large numbers of participants might be beyond your resources in terms of contacting them, interviewing them, and analyzing the large amount of data that would result.

Third, ask experienced researchers for their advice on this issue. For thesis and dissertation students, this is especially important. Ask the members of your committee what sample size they recommend given your purpose, method of research, and any other anticipated complexities that you may face in conducting the research.

Fourth, keep in mind that you may be forgiven for using a sample that is smaller than typical for your type of research if you are proposing to explore research purposes, questions, or hypotheses that have great promise for advancing knowledge and are likely to have important implications. Put another way, proposing to use a very small sample to study a mundane research question might doom your proposal when it is evaluated by others. A proposal on a compelling research question might be approved even if you have the resources and contacts to obtain only a small sample.

Despite the above discussion, many students are likely to feel that they have been left out to dry on this topic without being given some specific numbers, so some will be offered here with the understanding that they are to be regarded as *exceedingly rough* guidelines for sample sizes that might be used in studies of different types.[1]

- For *qualitative research*, consider proposing an initial sample with one to 20 participants. Keep in mind that qualitative researchers sometimes adjust their sample size as they gather data and see the need for more participants or find that additional par-

---

[1] These are very rough, so this material should not be cited in a proposal to justify a particular sample size.

ticipants are not adding to the discovery of information.

- For *survey research* on very large populations such as all citizens of a state, 800 or more participants might be proposed. (Professional pollsters often use 1,500.) To survey smaller populations, Table 1 at the end of this book provides suggested sample sizes that might be proposed.
- For *correlational research*, consider proposing to use 75 to 200 participants.
- For *experiments*, a sample size of 30 or less might be proposed if the administration of the treatments is time-consuming, expensive, or has poten-

tial for harm to participants. Otherwise, more than 30 is desirable.

- For *causal comparative research*, 30 or more might be proposed.

You may also remember from your statistics class that larger samples are more likely to yield statistically significant results than smaller samples. Thus, if you anticipate a small difference, which works against obtaining significance, consider proposing a large sample size to offset the small difference when you conduct significance tests.

Exercise for Topic 29

1. Examine the literature you have collected for use in your proposal. What is your estimate of the typical sample size used in published studies of the type you are planning?

2. Will you be proposing to use a sample size that is roughly the same as the one you named in response to question 1? If no, what sample size will you propose? Explain.

Part G

Proposing Instrumentation

Under the major heading "Method," you should have described your proposed sample under the subheading "Participants." Next, you need a subheading for "Instrumentation," which will describe how you intend to measure the variables in your study. In this part of the book, you will learn how to write this part of the proposal.

To make sure you are not getting lost, consider the outline in the following box, which shows the major headings and subheadings that are used in a typical research proposal.

    I. Introduction
   II. Literature Review*
  III. Method
        A. Participants
        B. Instrumentation   ←*You are here.*
        C. Procedures
  IV. Analysis
   V. Discussion**

*May be integrated with the Introduction.
**Followed by writing a title and an abstract as well as developing a timeline.

Notes

Topic 30

Qualitative Instrumentation

Qualitative research is more free-form than quantitative research largely because qualitative researchers emphasize obtaining information from the point of view of the participants (see Topic 12). Highly structured instruments (i.e., objective measurement procedures) are incompatible with this goal because they impose a structure that is likely to influence how respondents perceive a phenomenon and respond to it. In other words, the act of measurement can influence respondents, and the more detailed and specific the instrument is, the more likely it is to influence them.

To avoid this problem, qualitative researchers often use open-ended interviews (i.e., questions are asked but respondents are not provided with choices to use as answers). Typically, these are *semistructured*, meaning that some questions will be developed in advance with follow-up questions developed on the spot in light of participants' responses. If you will be proposing to use such an instrument, be as specific as possible about its contents and use. The following example shows how this might be done.

Example

The questions will be open-ended to avoid influencing participants' responses. Five prompting questions will be developed by the researcher for each of the areas specified in the research purpose stated earlier: (a) current position (likes and dislikes about the job and career path leading to the job), (b) external challenges and limitations to achievement on the job, and (c) success and failure on the job

(definition of, perceptions of capabilities, and achievements). All prompts will be pilot tested with a sample of five women who will *not* participate in the main study. The prompts that are most productive in terms of eliciting information and that the women in the pilot study seem most comfortable in responding to will be selected for the main study.

In the main study, all interviews will be conducted by this researcher (a middle-aged African American woman) either in the participants' homes or places of work as selected by the participants. After participants respond to the prompts selected on the basis of the pilot study, the interviewer will follow up with additional questions to explore information related to the purposes of this research. In addition, field notes will be taken on the setting for each interview, which will be used to describe the context in which the interviews were conducted.

All interviews will be audiotaped, and transcripts will be prepared by the researcher. Each participant will be sent a copy of the transcript of her interview and asked to review it for accuracy and for any additional information she might wish to add with hindsight.[1]

Of course, there can be many variations on this example. The main goal is to write a description that is as specific as possible while permitting you the flexibility that is required in qualitative research. Note that specificity may be required by instructors or funding agencies that will be evaluating your proposal.

---

[1] This example is based in part on the work of Richie, B. S., Fassinger, R. E., Linn, S. G., Johnson, J., Prosser, J., & Robinson, S. (1997). Persistence, connection and passion: A qualitative study of the career development of highly achieving African American–Black and White women. *Journal of Counseling Psychology, 44*, 133–148.

Another measurement technique often used by qualitative researchers is direct observation either as a *participant observer* (one who is participating as a member of a group while making observations) or as a *nonparticipant observer* (one who is making observations but is not participating). If you will be proposing direct observation, consider addressing the following issues in your proposal: (a) the *types* of behaviors you will be observing for, which should be determined by your research purposes, (b) who will make the observations, (c) when and where will the observations be made, (d) how the observations will be recorded, and (e) whether feedback on the first draft of the research report will be solicited from the participants. You should also address the issue of how long you will observe by discussing your *initial estimate*, which can be modified as needed while conducting the research.

Showing your readers that you have carefully considered your approach(es) to measurement in qualitative research will be a strength of your proposal.

Exercise for Topic 30

1. If you will be conducting qualitative research, will you be conducting interviews? Making observations? Using some other data collection method?

2. Write a description of the instrumentation you will use.

Topic 31

Proposing Published Instruments

There are two types of "published" instruments in the social and behavioral sciences. First, there are tests and scales published by commercial publishers. Typically, these have undergone extensive development and much is known about their characteristics such as their reliability and validity. Very often, they come with national norms that allow a comparison between the group you will be studying and a national norm group tested by the publisher.

Second, there are noncommercial "published" instruments. Usually, these are tests and scales that were developed by researchers for particular research purposes and are published in the sense that they appear in the journal articles reporting on their research or are available through test collection services.[1]

Obviously, an important advantage of proposing to use published instruments is that others have gone to considerable trouble to develop and refine them. In your proposal, you can summarize what is already known about them to help justify their selection for use in your proposed study. The following example shows how this might be done.

Example

The Donovan Depression Scale (Donovan, 1990) will be used in this study. It has been widely used in other studies of depression, including a number of recent studies (e.g., Doe, 1998; Johns, 1999; and Smith, 2000). Validity was established by the publisher by correlating the scale with other previously published measures of depression and anxiety. The correlations with the measures of depression were significantly higher than the correlations with anxiety, indicating adequate convergent-divergent validity. The test-retest reliability coefficient for this instrument was .79, indicating adequate temporal reliability. Coefficient alpha is reported by the publisher to be .80, indicating adequate internal consistency. The use of this instrument in the proposed study will allow an unconfounded comparison with the results of the numerous other studies in which this instrument has been used (see the literature review in this proposal).

The last sentence in this example is especially important. If you want to compare and contrast your results with those obtained in earlier research, you should consider proposing to use the instrument(s) that were employed in that research. For instance, suppose you find that your treatment for depression is superior to one previously reported in the literature. If you use a *different* instrument, you will have confounded the comparison. That is, you will have used a different instrument and a different treatment than previously used, so either could be the explanation for the observed difference in results.

The main reason for *not* using a published instrument is a mismatch between your research purposes, questions, or hypotheses and the available published instruments. This happens more often

---

[1] The ETS Test Collection describes and provides availability information on more than 10,000 commercial and noncommercial tests and research instruments. It can be accessed via the Internet at this address: WWW.ericae.net/testcol.htm#ETSTF

than you might think. For example, suppose you want to measure just a very limited number of algebra skills and all the published tests cover much broader areas of algebra. Or suppose you need to measure attitudes toward a new policy recommendation that has not been studied before, so none of the available attitude measures are direct hits. In situations like these, you should consider proposing to develop a new instrument specifically for use in your study, a possibility that is discussed in the next topic.

Exercise for Topic 31

Directions: If you will be using more than one published instrument, answer the following questions once for each instrument (e.g., answer the questions twice if you will be using two published instruments).

1. Will you be proposing to use a published instrument? If yes, name it and give its source.

2. If yes to question 1, write a statement describing the proposed instrument, incorporating into your statement information that is already known about it.

Topic 32

Proposing New Instruments

At the end of the previous topic, you were advised that there should be a close match between your research purposes, questions, or hypotheses and the measuring instruments you propose to use. When there are no published instruments that match closely, you will need to develop new instruments.

When proposing to develop new instruments for use in your research, it is usually insufficient to make a simple statement such as, "A new measure of parents' attitudes toward school will be developed." Instead, you should address the following issues in a more comprehensive statement, covering at a minimum: (1) why a new measure is needed, (2) what its underlying structure will be, that is, what broad areas will be covered, (3) what types of items will be used, and (4) how it will be developed and refined. The following example shows how this might be done.

Example

A new measure of parents' attitudes toward their children's schools will be developed for use in this study. A new measure is needed because none of the existing scales address attitudes toward the unique aspects of the power structure in newly formed public charter schools, which is the primary focus of this proposed research. The new scale will cover three areas and have the following structure. First, there will be 10 items on the increased power and influence of parents in school decision making. Each item will consist of a statement that respondents will rate on a five-point scale from 5 (strongly agree) to 1 (strongly disagree). An illustrative item is:

"Parents are too emotionally involved with their children to be good decision makers in setting school policies regarding discipline." Approximately 10 additional items of the same type will be on the increased power and influence of teachers in school decision making, and an additional 10 will be on the decreased power and influence of school principals.

An initial pool of 15 statements for each of the three areas that will be covered by the instrument will be brainstormed by three graduate students who have been active in the charter school movement. These will be reviewed by two professors who have experience in attitude scale development and are knowledgeable of this movement. The pool of items will also be pilot tested with a sample of five parents who will *not* be participants in the main study. Each parent will be asked to read each statement aloud and describe his or her reasons for selecting a choice from 5 to 1. This "think-aloud" technique will help identify statements that parents find to be vague or ambiguous.

The final selection of 10 of the 15 statements for each area of the instrument will be made by the researcher in light of the feedback from the professors and the pilot test with parents.

Note that students planning research for their doctoral dissertation and those seeking major research funding may be expected to propose conducting full-scale reliability and validity studies on their new instruments before their use in the main study. Also note that even for thesis research or research being proposed for a class project, the committee members or instructors who are reviewing the proposal may want to see at least a first draft of all the items before approving the proposal. Finally, note that showing in your proposal that a new instrument will be developed with care, including pilot testing and revision in light of feedback from others, will be a major strength of your research proposal.

Exercise for Topic 32

Directions: If you will be using more than one new instrument, answer the following question once for each instrument (e.g., answer the question twice if you will be using two new instruments).

1. Will you be developing a new instrument for use in your proposed research? If yes, write a statement covering the four items listed in this topic. (See the numbered list of four items in the first column on the previous page.)

Topic 33

Proposing to Measure Demographics

In your section on instrumentation, you should address the issue of which demographics (i.e., background characteristics) you will measure. Demographic information will help give your readers a picture of the participants in your research, and a statement regarding demographics should be included in proposals for both quantitative and qualitative research.

Keep in mind that some (if not many) participants might find demographic questions intrusive or objectionable, so it is best to ask for only those that are related to your research purposes, questions, or hypotheses. For example, a demographic question on "religion" would probably be inappropriate in a study on learning mathematics using manipulative materials.

Often in a proposal, it is adequate to make a simple statement that names the demographic variables. Example 1 shows such a statement.

Example 1
Demographic information on gender, age, ethnicity, and highest level of education completed will be collected.

If you are expected to be more explicit about how you will collect demographic information, provide more details as illustrated in Example 2.

Example 2
The last section of the questionnaire will request demographic information on gender, age, ethnicity, and highest level of education completed. This section will be clearly

marked as "optional," with a statement to the effect that it is needed for statistical purposes and will help the researchers understand more about the participants. Since "age" is potentially sensitive among this group of adults, ages will be presented in grouped intervals (e.g., 18–29, 30–39) so that participants will not be asked to indicate their specific ages. "Ethnicity" is also potentially sensitive and poses problems in wording (e.g., Latina vs. Chicana). Thus, the question for this variable will be open-ended without choices provided by the researcher, which will allow respondents to use terms of their own choice.[1]

When using children as participants, consider whether it is appropriate to ask them for the demographic information you desire. Young children may not be valid sources of information on variables such as ethnicity, household income, and religion. In addition, it might be unethical and insensitive to collect this information from children without their parents' permission. In your proposal, you should address how you will collect such information about the children. Teachers might have solid information on the children's ethnicity. Parents might be willing to disclose their income. In whatever manner you plan to collect such information, spell it out in your proposal.

---

[1] For more information on collecting information on sensitive demographic variables, including the use of choices for soliciting information on race/ethnicity, see Patten, M. L. (1998). *Questionnaire Research: A Practical Guide*. Los Angeles: Pyrczak Publishing.

Exercise for Topic 33

1. What types of demographic information do you plan to collect?

2. Write a brief statement naming the demographic variables. (See Example 1 in this topic.)

3. If you are expected to write a more detailed statement regarding demographics, write it here. (See Example 2 in this topic.)

Topic 34
Ethical Issues in Measurement

Measuring in order to gather data for research purposes often raises ethical issues. When this is the case, you should explicitly address the matter in your proposal.

First, you should plan to protect your participants' *privacy*. By collecting *anonymous* responses to questionnaires and other instruments, you can provide them with this protection. Thus, if you will be providing anonymity, you should state that in your proposal.

Sometimes having the participants remain anonymous will not be possible. First, you may need to know their identities in order to match them with other sources of information. For example, to achieve your research purpose, you might need to match individual participants' responses to an instrument with their GPAs on school records. In addition, some measurement techniques are inherently not anonymous such as face-to-face interviews or direct observation of behavior. When this is the case, the best you can offer is *confidentiality*, that is, sharing the information you collect with only those who need to know in order to conduct the research. The following example shows how this issue might be addressed in a research proposal.

Example
Because it will be necessary to match individual participants' scores on this measure of risk-taking tendencies with their information on their safety record contained in their personnel files, participants will be asked to write their names on the answer sheets. They will be advised that the information will remain confidential. To assure that this is the case, the answer sheets will be collected by this researcher and kept in a secure location until the safety-record information from the personnel files has been recorded on the answer sheets by the researcher. Once this is done, the researcher will physically remove (cut out) the names of the respondents and archive the answer sheets in a secure location.

As you plan your instrumentation, you should also consider how to provide *protection from psychological harm*. Suppose you plan to interview women who recently survived a rape experience. Since the interview may cause trauma, you should inform them in advance of the topic of the interviews, get their consent, and assure them that they are free to withdraw from the interview at any time without penalty. Some researchers investigating such sensitive matters have even made available psychological counseling on a 24-hour basis for a limited amount of time (such as for a week after the data collection) in order to help participants who were unintentionally harmed by participation in the research.

Sometimes the potential for harm may be rather subtle. For instance, you might need to administer an attitude-toward-math scale to third graders. If you do this during classroom time, you might be depriving the students of other instructional activities that will benefit them directly. (Most research benefits participants only very indirectly.) Even if you consider this a minor matter, the school officials from whom you will need to get permission to conduct the research might view it differently and deny you access.

Most universities and other research institutions and agencies require that research proposals be reviewed by a committee that will consider the issues we are considering in this topic. This committee is likely to pay special attention to how you will be measuring and whether participants are adequately protected. Thus, it is a good idea to explicitly discuss ethical issues in your proposal.

Note that such committees are usually also responsible for reviewing your informed consent form (a printed explanation of the research for potential respondents), so you should get a copy of your institution's guidelines on preparing such a form early in the research planning process.

The next section of this book deals with research procedures you will propose. Since these can also harm participants, we will consider ethical issues again in Topic 37.

Exercise for Topic 34

1. Do you anticipate that your measurement procedures will raise any ethical issues? Explain.

2. If you answered yes to question 1, write a description that explicitly addresses the issues, including how you propose to minimize them.

Part H

Proposing Procedures

Under the major heading "Method," you should have described your proposed sample under the subheading "Participants" and your measurement techniques under the subheading "Instrumentation." The last subheading under "Method" typically is "Procedures." Under this subheading, you should describe any physical acts you will perform to execute the research.

To make sure you are not getting lost, consider the outline in the following box, which shows the major headings and subheadings that are used in a typical research proposal.

> I.   Introduction
> II. Literature Review*
> III. Method
>   A. Participants
>   B. Instrumentation
>   C. Procedures   ←*You are here.*
> IV. Analysis
> V.   Discussion**

*May be integrated with the Introduction.
**Followed by writing a title and an abstract as well as developing a timeline.

Notes

Topic 35

Nonexperimental Procedures

In the "Procedures" subsection, you should describe the physical things you plan to do in order to conduct your study. Usually, you should address these issues: what you will do, when you will do it, and how long you will do it.[1] This should be done even for seemingly simple methodological studies such as mailed surveys, which is illustrated in Example 1.

Example 1

Postcards that describe the upcoming study will be mailed to all names on the mailing list. These cards will stress the importance of the study and ask recipients to watch their mail for the questionnaire that will be arriving soon. Previous research indicates that prior notification by postcard has a positive effect on response rate (Doe, 1999).

One week after the postcards are mailed, the questionnaires with a cover letter and stamped envelope will be mailed. Two weeks later, all potential respondents will be mailed a second copy of the questionnaire and envelope with a cover letter that stresses the importance of the study and asks them to ignore the second mailing if they have already responded to the first one.

The postcard, cover letters, and questionnaire will be reviewed by all members of the thesis committee and revised, if necessary, prior to mailing.

If participants will be physically present while you gather the data, you should describe the location, what will be done in their presence, and how long the interaction is anticipated to last. Example

2 is the proposed procedure for an observational study of mother-child communication.

Example 2

When each mother-child dyad arrives at the Child Development Laboratory, they will be taken by the researcher to a private room, and the mother and child will be asked to be seated at a small table. At that point, a beeper will go off, and the researcher will state that she is needed in another part of the laboratory but will return shortly. Before leaving the room, she will remove the Lollipop Puzzle (described below) from a drawer and offer it to the child to play with while waiting for the researcher's return. After leaving the room, the researcher will then observe the mother and child through a one-way mirror and record relevant aspects of their communication on the Communicative Dissonance Direct Observation Checklist described above under Instrumentation. At the end of the ten-minute observation period, the researcher will return to the room, praise the child for making progress in putting the puzzle together, and....

It is a good idea to propose that procedures such as those in Example 2 will be pilot tested and revised as needed before being used in the main study. In a pilot study, for example, you might learn that the task you plan to provide (the puzzle) does not stimulate sufficient mother-child communication for you to gather the data you need or that ten minutes is too long or too short a period given the task.

Providing detailed information on procedures will allow a proper evaluation of your proposal.

---

[1] Qualitative researchers should describe *anticipated* procedures since they might modify them during the course of their research.

Exercise for Topic 35

1. Write a detailed description of your procedures, have it reviewed by other students or instructors, and revise it. (If you will be conducting an *experiment*, you should wait until after you have read Topic 36 to write the description.)

Topic 36

Procedures in Experiments

A classic, simple experiment consists of two groups that are given different treatments. Your first obligation under "Procedures" is to describe how individuals will arrive at their group membership. If they will be assigned at random to groups, which is highly desirable, you should explicitly say so. On the other hand, if they are already in groups (such as students already enrolled in one high school to be compared with those enrolled in another one), this should be stated and any information on their comparability should be provided. For instance, are the achievement levels at the two high schools comparable? Do the students in the two schools come from similar socioeconomic levels?

If you will not be using random assignment to groups, it is good to acknowledge that this will not be done followed by a statement on why you are not proposing it. Often, this is because you do not have sufficient control over or cooperation from participants.

Your next obligation is to describe in as much detail as possible what will be done to the experimental group. For very complex treatments such as a year-long new curriculum program in first-grade mathematics, you might describe it in sufficient detail so that your readers can visualize the *types* of things that will be done and refer them to a published source (such as a curriculum guide) for details on day-to-day activities. An alternative

for very complex treatments is to once again describe the *types* of things that will be done and prepare a detailed appendix on the treatment to include at the end of your proposal. The following example, which is only a partial description of an experimental treatment, illustrates the level of detail that might be desirable in a proposal for an experiment.

Example

In the experimental condition, each student will be taught to recognize each target word by using flashcards. Each word, printed on an index card, will be shown to the student to be read aloud. (See Appendix A for a complete list of the target words.) If the student cannot say the word, it will then be shown in a two-word phrase, which will be written on the back of the card (e.g., for "lemonade," the two-word phrase will be "lemonade drink"). This training will continue until a student can recognize each word in one second or until 20 minutes have passed, which is the amount of time that will be allocated to each training session. After training, with the flashcards, each student will be given....[1]

Next, you should describe what will be done to the control or comparison group. Note that whatever happens to them during the course of the experiment will be important for interpreting the resulting data. For instance, for the control group in the example, will the students receive their normal reading lessons?

---

[1] This example is loosely based on the work of Tan, A. & Nicholson, T. (1997). Flashcards revisited: Training poor readers to read words faster improves their comprehension of text. *Journal of Educational Psychology, 89,* 276–288.

Will these lessons contain the same words as the target words on the flashcards? If the answer is "yes" to both of these questions, the experimental comparison is very different from one in which the control children are given a free-play period with no reading instruction.

Sometimes experiments are conducted using a single group. For example, a group might receive normal praise for a while, then increased praise, followed by the reintroduction of normal praise. When proposing such an experiment, state how long each condition is expected to last and specifically what will be done in each.

Since the purpose of an experiment is to determine the effects of *treatments* on some outcome measure(s), a detailed description of the treatments is essential in a good proposal for experimental research.

Exercise for Topic 36

1. If you will be conducting an experiment, write a first draft of the description of the experimental treatment.

2. Write a description of what will be done to the control group while the experimental group is receiving its treatment.

3. Do you anticipate referring your readers to published sources for more information on the treatment(s)? Do you anticipate including an appendix with detailed information on the treatment(s)? Explain.

Topic 37
Ethical Issues and Procedures

In Topic 34, you were advised that the act of measurement may pose ethical problems if participants' rights to *privacy* are not adequately protected. In addition, you were advised that measurement might cause *psychological* harm and stress.

Likewise, the procedures you use might cause psychological harm. For example, suppose a confederate (someone working for you as a researcher) is going to fake a physical assault on another confederate while the true participants in the study are onlookers. Your goal is to determine the extent to which the participants will intervene to stop the assault. As you can imagine, merely witnessing such an assault might be quite disturbing. In addition, when participants fail to intervene, they will gain insights about themselves that may cause self-doubt and worry. To complicate matters, this study also holds the potential for *physical harm* since a participant might physically intervene and get hurt in the process.

Sometimes research projects that clearly have the potential for psychological and physical harm are ethically conducted *if* the participants were fully informed of the nature of the research and the potential for harm and then freely agreed to participate. However, for the study we are considering, if potential participants are informed that the physical attack will be a fake attack, the experiment would lose its validity. As a general rule, novice researchers should avoid proposing such highly problematic research projects.

Of course, the potential for harm can be subtle and difficult to predict in advance. For instance, a researcher at a university proposed lightly brushing just inside students' nostrils with a cotton swab in order to obtain sample cultures. One member of the institutional review board raised the obvious concern that the person using the swabs might not be properly trained, insert it too far, and harm the participants. Another raised the somewhat less obvious issue of sterility. Could the researcher assure the committee that the swabs would be sterile? Even if they were, participants might *perceive* that they were not. For instance, a participant who came down with the flu the next day might accuse the researcher of giving him or her the flu. After this discussion, the committee recommended that the cultures be collected by a registered nurse. The proposal was cheerfully rewritten to include this provision, and the proposal was approved.

The example we have just considered illustrates the value of institutional review boards in helping to protect participants. Before submitting your proposal to such a committee, try to brainstorm with others what types of things might go wrong. Then, address them explicitly in your proposal—with attention to measures you will take to help protect your participants.

If you will be submitting your proposal to a review committee, do so as soon as possible. Understandably, the committee might not be willing to make a determination before seeing the whole proposal, but often there is a university administrator who coordinates the work of the committee who might be willing to give you some preliminary advice based on his or her experience working with the committee.

Exercise for Topic 37

1. Are you aware of any potential for psychological harm your procedures might pose? Explain.

2. Are you aware of any potential for physical harm your procedures might pose? Explain.

3. If you answered yes to questions 1 or 2, write a statement addressing them for inclusion in the "Procedures" subsection of your proposal.

Part I

Proposing Methods of Analysis

Your next step is to propose a method of analysis. In this part of the book, we will start with some guidelines for analyzing qualitative data. Then, we will consider statistical methods, limiting ourselves to those statistics commonly taught in an introductory statistics class. Those who have taken more advanced classes will have additional statistical methods at their disposal.

Important Notes

Topics 39 through 42 should be read in sequence because some of the statistical terms defined in earlier topics are *not* redefined in later ones.

Unless you are thoroughly grounded in basic statistical methods, you may find some of the material in Topics 39 through 42 difficult to follow. If you are in this situation, consider either taking more coursework in statistics or locating a statistics tutor or consultant to assist you in writing your proposed method of analysis. Having a fuzzy or unsuitable proposal for the analysis of data can be a fatal flaw in a research proposal.

> I.   Introduction
> II. Literature Review*
> III. Method
>   A. Participants
>   B. Instrumentation
>   C. Procedures
> IV. Analysis   ←*You are here.*
> V.   Discussion**

*May be integrated with the Introduction.
**Followed by writing a title and an abstract as well as developing a timeline.

Notes

Topic 38

Qualitative Analysis

Specific plans should be made for the analysis of qualitative data. Careful, systematic plans for this stage of the research help distinguish serious qualitative scholars from those who confuse qualitative research with casual everyday observation.

Typically, the proposed method of analysis should cover (a) who will analyze the data, (b) which method(s) of analysis will be employed, and (c) the major steps that will be followed. Examples 1 and 2 illustrate how this might be done.[1]

Example 1

The data analytic procedures suggested for consensual qualitative research (Hill et al., 1997) will be applied by the three members of the research team (three white female graduate students in clinical psychology, average age 26.4).

In the first step, each team member will develop an overall "start list" of descriptive domains (clusters of units of meaning contained in the interview transcripts). Then the team will meet and confer until a consensus is reached on how to break the interviews into domains.

The second step will be to independently construct core ideas for each domain. The team will meet and arrive at a consensus on the core ideas.

Next, the work of the team to this point along with the original transcripts will be sent to an outside auditor (a middle-aged male professor of psychology). His task will be to review....

Next....

In Example 2, the steps are numbered, a feature that helps readers follow the proposed process when the description of the proposed method of analysis is lengthy.

Example 2

Tapes will be transcribed verbatim and checked for accuracy by a second individual.

Analysis of the transcribed interviews will follow a modified pattern outlined by Giorgi (1985, 1989). The essence of this pattern is to break down transcribed interviews into units that can be more easily analyzed. These units are called *meaning units*. This analysis will be conducted by the researcher under the direct supervision of his thesis advisor.

The analysis will consist of the following seven steps:

Step 1: Since it is important to get an overall sense of each interview, each one will be listened to and read three or four times before the analysis is conducted.

Step 2: The researcher will read each transcribed interview to identify experienced shifts in meaning (meaning units)....

Step 3: Meaning units will be examined for relevancy to the research purpose. Irrelevant meaning units will be discarded....

Step 4: Integration of the meaning units will be accomplished by....

Step 5: The meaning units will be translated into psychologically relevant meanings by....

Step 6: Based on the results of Step 5, derived meanings will be integrated in a third-

---

[1] Example 1 is based loosely on the work of Williams, E. N., Soeprapto, E., Like, K., Touradji, P., Hess, S., & Hill, C. (1998). Perceptions of serendipity: Career paths of prominent academic women in counseling psychology. *Journal of Counseling Psychology, 45*, 379–389. Example 2 is loosely based on Worthen, V. & McNeill, B. W. (1996). A phenomenological investigation of "good" supervision events. *Journal of Counseling Psychology, 43*, 25–34.

person narrative retelling....

Step 7: This final step will refine the description into its most distilled and concise form by....

An outside auditor (a professor with experience in qualitative research methodology) will review the results of Step 7. Any disagreements between the researcher and auditor will be resolved through discussion, with the goal of reaching consensus.

Notice that in both examples, more than one person will be involved in the analysis, and in both cases, an outside auditor will review the results of the preliminary analysis. If you have the contacts and resources to involve other people, it is recommended that you propose to do so.

Exercise for Topic 38

1. If you will be conducting qualitative analysis, will you have other researchers help (or supervise) you during the analysis? Will you use an auditor? Explain.

2. Write a proposal for the analysis of your qualitative data. (Consider preparing a step-by-step description as illustrated by the examples in this topic.)

Topic 39

Analysis of Demographics

You undoubtedly proposed to collect data on the demographics (i.e., background characteristics) of your participants. (See Topic 33.) Whether your proposed research is qualitative or quantitative, you should state in your proposal how you will analyze this data.

Many demographics are measured at what is known as the *nominal level of measurement*. This is jargon for saying that the participants were put in categories that have word names (as opposed to scores). For example, *gender* is a nominal variable with the categories (in words) of "males" and "females." Likewise, political affiliation is a nominal variable with categories such as "Republican," "Democrat," "Reform," and "Independent."

Many other demographics are measured at the *equal interval level* (known as *interval* and *ratio levels* in statistics classes).[1] At this level, participants are classified on a numerical scale in which all score points are equally distant from each other. For example, *age* is measured at the equal interval level because the difference between any points on the scale (such as the difference between 2 years and 3 years) is the same as the distance between any other two points (such as the difference between 20 years

and 21 years). Other common demographics measured at this level are household income (measured in dollars), years of education completed, and number of children. Likewise, scores obtained using objective tests are usually assumed to be equal interval.

Often demographics at both the nominal and equal interval levels will be measured in the same study. The following example shows a proposed analysis for this situation.

Example

For the demographic data for variables measured at the nominal level (gender and ethnicity), percentages will be computed and reported along with the numbers of cases in each category. For equal interval data (age and number of years abusing drugs), means and standard deviations will be computed. If the distributions for either of these variables is highly skewed, medians and interquartile ranges will also be computed and reported.

If you have two or more distinct groups in your study such as participants who abuse marijuana and participants who abuse heroin, you could propose to report their demographics separately. For instance, we could add the words "separately for each of the two groups in this study" immediately after the word "category" in the example.

Sometimes scores are grouped when demographics are measured. For instance, income might be measured by having participants check off the income group (e.g., $0–$9,999, $10,000–$19,000, etc.) to which they belong. These groups

---

[1] You may recall from your statistics class that the *ordinal* level of measurement puts participants in rank order. This level of measurement is seldom used when collecting demographic data. Should you have such data, consider proposing the calculation of medians and interquartile ranges.

are known as *score intervals*. For such data, you should propose to calculate the percentage for each income interval and report them with the numbers of cases in each interval.

If some of the terminology in this section is only vaguely familiar to you, consult your statistics textbook to refresh your memory. If you need a quick, non-technical review of introductory statistics,

Making Sense of Statistics: A Conceptual Overview by Fred Pyrczak (Los Angeles: Pyrczak Publishing) is recommended.

Note that it is not usually necessary to name the computer program you will be using or to show the formulas to be used *unless* you are required to do so for instructional purposes.

Exercise for Topic 39

1. Which demographic variables, if any, will you be measuring at the nominal level?

2. Which demographic variables, if any, will you be measuring at the equal interval level (either interval or ratio scales)?

3. Write a first draft of a paragraph in which you propose the analysis of the demographic data you will be collecting.

Topic 40

Relationships: Nominal

Often, a research purpose, question, or hypothesis requires the examination of relationships between nominal variables. Nominal variables are those that put participants into "named" categories such as the variable called gender, which puts participants into the categories "male" and "female." Example 1 shows a research purpose concerning the relationship between two nominal variables: gender (male vs. female) and completion (completed vs. not completed).

Example 1

This study will examine the relationship between gender and successful completion of a behavioral drug rehabilitation program.

Example 2 shows a proposed method of analysis for the research question in Example 1.

Example 2

To examine the relationship between gender and successful completion of the behavioral drug rehabilitation program, a two-way contingency table with percentages and numbers of cases shown in each cell will be prepared. The statistical significance of the differences in the table will be tested at the .05 level with a chi square test.[1]

In Example 2, the term "two-way contingency" table is used. In case you have forgotten what this is, Example 3 shows one with some hypothetical data.

Example 3

	Program completed	Program not completed
Male	33.3% ($n = 10$)	66.7% ($n = 20$)
Female	50.0% ($n = 20$)	50.0% ($n = 20$)

Also note the use of the term "at the .05 level" in Example 2. This means that if the probability that the relationship would be created by random error is 5 in 100 *or less*, the relationship will be declared to be statistically significant. The .05 level is the most common one used in research proposals.

Note that the *chi square test* is designed for use when determining the significance of the relationship between two nominal variables. Of course, you are not restricted to examining only one relationship in your proposed study. Frequently, researchers have a "key variable" such as gender that will be related to a number of other variables such as (a) gender and program completion, (b) gender and returning for a follow-up examination, (c) gender and becoming employed, and so on.

Also note that you are not restricted to nominal variables that have only two categories each. Example 4 shows a contingency table for a variable in which one variable (experience) has three categories. The relationship between the two variables in this table should also be tested for significance with a chi square test.

---

[1] The chi square test will determine only whether the relationship is statistically significant. To describe the strength of the relationship, you might propose to calculate a coefficient of contingency or Cramér's statistic (ϕ').

Example 4

	Highly experienced	Somewhat experienced	Not at all experienced
Male	25.0% $(n = 100)$	25.0% $(n = 100)$	50.0% $(n = 200)$
Female	44.4% $(n = 40)$	33.3% $(n = 30)$	22.2% $(n = 20)$

In the next Topic, we will consider examining relationships between two equal interval (i.e., interval and ratio) variables.

Exercise for Topic 40

1. If you will be examining the relationship between nominal variables, write a first draft of your proposed analysis here.

Topic 41
Relationships: Equal Interval

Often, a research purpose, question, or hypothesis requires the examination of the relationship between two equal interval (i.e., interval or ratio) variables.[1] Here are some examples of research questions that do this:

- To what extent do reading readiness test scores obtained in kindergarten predict reading achievement test scores obtained at the end of first grade?

- How strongly correlated are anxiety and depression?

- Are College Board SAT scores or high school GPA a better predictor of college freshmen GPA?

Note that the last research question requires that two relationships be examined: (1) the relationship between SAT scores and college GPA and (2) the relationship between high school GPA and college GPA. The variable with the stronger relationship with college GPA is the better predictor.

The standard statistical tool for examining relationships between two equal interval measures is the Pearson product-moment correlation coefficient. You may recall that its symbol is r and that it ranges from −1.00 (perfect inverse relationship) through 0.00 (no relationship) to 1.00 (perfect direct relationship).

The following example shows how the analysis might be proposed for a study with two equal interval variables.

Example

First, the distributions on the Doe Depression Scale and the Smith Manifest Anxiety Scale will be examined. Based on the literature on these measures when used with samples of college students, it is assumed that there will be considerable variation in both distributions and that neither will be significantly skewed. If these assumptions are correct, the analysis will proceed as follows. First, means and standard deviations will be computed as measures of central tendency and variability, respectively. Then, a Pearson product-moment correlation coefficient will be computed for the relationship between the scores on the two measures. The resulting correlation coefficient will be tested for statistical significance at the .05 level. If it is significant, the value of the coefficient of determination (r^2) will be computed to aid in interpreting the magnitude of the relationship.

If you will be correlating a number of variables, you might propose preparing a correlation matrix, which is a table that shows the relationships among all pairs of variables.

If you wish to predict the scores of individuals on one variable from another variable (such as predicting college GPA from high school GPA), you should propose conducting simple linear regression, which will yield the values needed to make such predictions.

If you wish to determine how well one variable can be predicted from a *combination* of other variables (such as

---

[1] Note that most physical measurements as well as scores on objective tests or scales are assumed to be equal interval.

predicting college GPA from high school GPA *and* SAT scores), you should propose to conduct a multiple linear regression.

As you can see, there are many options in correlation (including ones not even mentioned above such as factor analysis). While you will be able to conduct and interpret simple correlational studies based on what you learned in an introductory statistics class, for more advanced methods, you will need a course in advanced correlational techniques.

Exercise for Topic 41

1. Do you anticipate proposing to use correlational techniques? If yes, which variables will be correlated with each other?

2. If you will be conducting a correlational study, write a first draft of your proposed method of analysis.

Topic 42

Group Differences

Often, a research purpose, question, or hypothesis requires examination of the relationship between a nominal variable and an equal interval variable. Here is an example of a research question that does this:

- Is individual competition for prizes or participation in cooperative learning groups more effective in promoting achievement in first-grade mathematics? (Note: Placement in either an individual competition condition or in a cooperative learning condition is a *nominal* variable. Mathematics achievement is usually measured with an objective test, which is assumed to be *equal interval*.)

To examine the relationship between the two variables we are considering, the usual method of analysis is based on a comparison of *average group differences*. That is, if there is a difference between the averages of the two groups on a mathematics test, then there is a relationship between how they were treated (individual competition vs. cooperative learning) and their achievement in mathematics. Example 1 illustrates a proposed method of analysis for this.

Example 1

Assuming that the distribution of scores is not significantly skewed, the analysis will proceed as follows. First, for each student, a change score will be computed by subtracting the pretest score from the posttest score. Then, means and standard deviations will be computed separately for pretest, posttest, and change scores for each group. Finally, the significance of the difference between the two mean change scores will be determined at the .05 level with a two-tailed t test for independent groups.

The example we have just considered is based on an experiment with a pretest and a posttest. The relationship between a nominal variable and an equal interval variable can also be examined in a nonexperimental study, as illustrated by this research purpose:

- The purpose of this research is to compare the trust-in-authority reported by three groups of teenage boys: (1) those who were physically abused, (2) those who were sexually abused, and (3) those who were not abused. Trust-in-authority will be measured with an objective self-report measure developed by Doe (1999).

The nominal variable (abuse) has three categories (physical, sexual, and no-abuse), so the analysis will require the computation of three means and standard deviations, as indicated in Example 2. Note that trust was measured only once (not as a pretest followed by a posttest).

Example 2

Assuming that the distribution of scores is not significantly skewed, the analysis will proceed as follows. First, the means and standard deviations of the trust scores will be computed for the three groups of boys. The differences among the three means will be tested with a one-way ANOVA with p set at .05. If this is statistically significant, individual pairs of means will be tested for significance using Scheffé's test (a multiple comparisons test).

If you will be measuring two nominal variables (such as gender and abuse status) and one equal interval variable (such as trust-in-authority), you should propose a two-way ANOVA, which will allow you to examine the interactive effects of the two nominal variables on trust.

Exercise for Topic 42

1. Will you be examining differences among groups? If so, name the groups.

2. Will there be pretests and posttests or only one test for each participant?

3. If you will be measuring one or more nominal variables (to form groups) and comparing equal interval measurements for the groups, write a proposed method of analysis here.

Part J

Concluding Tasks

After you have proposed a method of analysis for the data you plan to collect, you should wrap up the proposal with a discussion section, give the proposal a title, prepare an abstract of the proposal, develop a timeline, and have the first draft of your proposal reviewed. These tasks are discussed in this part of the book.

> I.   Introduction
> II.   Literature Review*
> III.   Method
>   A. Participants
>   B. Instrumentation
>   C. Procedures
> IV.   Analysis
> V.   Discussion**   ←*You are here.*

*May be integrated with the Introduction.
**Followed by writing a title and an abstract as well as developing
  a timeline.

Notes

Topic 43

Writing a Discussion Section

The body of the proposal should end with a discussion section. Consider beginning this section with a *summary* of the material that preceded it. While it may seem redundant to do this, keep in mind that many readers read quickly and may have skipped over important ideas (and this is your chance to present them again). Other readers may have lost the big picture while considering the details (and this is your chance to help them refocus). If you write a summary, emphasize why your problem area is important and how your particular research purposes, questions, or hypotheses will help to advance knowledge of the problem area in which you are proposing to work.

After the summary part of the discussion, consider discussing the *limitations* of your research methodology. For example, are you proposing to use a limited sample, or do you know of certain flaws in your instruments? Generally, it is best to acknowledge these explicitly so that your reader will know that you know what is ideal but are working under real-life constraints. Example 1 shows part of a discussion of limitations.

Example 1

The small sample size that is being proposed brings into question the potential representativeness of the participants. All clients and therapists will be European American from one geographical region. Furthermore, clients who agree to participate in the study may differ in important respects from clients who do not, which suggests the possibility of self-selection. Finally, only clients who are still in

therapy will be interviewed, and thus this study will not determine the perspectives of those who will have already terminated therapy. Clients who terminated may have left for a variety of reasons, one of which could be their experiences with the treatment that will be investigated in this study. Given these limitations, it will be necessary to exercise caution when generalizing from the results of the study.[1]

Consider ending your discussion section with a statement regarding the possible *implications*. Typically, implications address how individuals and organizations will be able to use the results by answering questions such as: Will the results help professionals better understand the phenomena that you plan to investigate? Will it help them formulate better theories? Will it help them provide better services to their clients and students? Example 2 shows part of such a discussion.

Example 2

Despite the limitations noted above, this study will provide the first test of the Dickens' grief therapy model in a sample of African American women. As such, it will help therapists understand the applicability of the model for working with such individuals when they are grieving the loss of a significant other. In addition, this study will provide insights into....

A detailed statement regarding possible implications is a strong way to end a proposal.

---

[1] This example is based loosely on material in Knox, S., Hess, S. A., Petersen, D. A., & Hill, C. E. (1997). A qualitative analysis of client perceptions of the effects of helpful therapist self-disclosure in long-term therapy. *Journal of Counseling Psychology, 44,* 274–283.

Exercise for Topic 43

1. Will you begin the discussion section with a summary? If yes, write a first draft of it.

2. Will you discuss the methodological limitations of your study? If yes, write a first draft of your discussion.

3. Write a first draft of a discussion of possible implications of your study.

Topic 44

Giving the Proposal a Title

Writing a title should be done with care since it is the first thing that most readers will consider when reviewing your proposal.

One of the most important principles in writing a title is to avoid the temptation to be clever. Engaging in empirical research is a serious matter, and your proposal deserves a serious title.

When writing the title, reexamine your research purposes, questions, or hypotheses to identify the main variables. These should be referred to in the title. Example 1 shows a research purpose and a corresponding title.

Example 1
Research purpose: To explore the relationship between self-reported altruism and the decision to donate one's organs.
Corresponding title: An Investigation of the Relationship Between Altruism and the Decision to Make Organ Donations

Notice that the title is *not* a sentence and does *not* end with a period. These are appropriate characteristics of a title for empirical research.

If there are many variables in your purpose, question, or hypothesis, consider referring to them by *type*. For example, if you are proposing to study 12 personality variables as they are exhibited by highly achieving women in sociology, refer to "personality traits" in the title instead of naming all 12 variables, as is done in Example 2.

Example 2
Personality Traits of Highly Achieving Women in Sociology: A Research Proposal

Notice that Example 2 ends with the subtitle "A Research Proposal," which could be added to any main title unless your title page already has this phrase on it elsewhere.

For an experiment or causal comparative study, the usual form for a title is "The Effects of A on B" or "The Effectiveness of A in producing changes in B," or "The Influence of A on B." Example 3 contains two titles. The first one is for an experiment, and the second one is for a causal comparative study.

Example 3
The Effects of Computer-Assisted Instruction on the Mathematics Achievement of Low-Achieving Second Grade Students

The Influence of Birth Order on the Development of Homosexuality in Adolescent Males

Finally, avoid stating your anticipated results in the title. While you may discuss the results you anticipate when you introduce a hypothesis in your proposal, they seldom belong in the title. Example 4 illustrates this.

Example 4
Poor title because it states anticipated results: Welfare Mothers Trained with the Wisconsin Program Should Be More Employable Than Control Mothers

Improved title: The Effects of the Wisconsin Program on the Employability of Welfare Mothers

Exercise for Topic 44

1. Write a tentative title for your research proposal, following the guidelines in this topic.

Topic 45

Preparing an Abstract

An abstract is a summary that provides an overview of the proposal. When there are many competing proposals (such as for research funding), preparing a good abstract is exceedingly important since some reviewers may make a first-pass and eliminate certain proposals based on the abstract alone. For example, if the funding agency is concentrating on inner-city adolescents and your abstract fails to mention this group, it may not get further consideration.

For many academic purposes (such as a term project), a short abstract (say 150–200 words) is adequate. You should check your institution's or instructor's requirements regarding length. If you find that you are required to write a very short abstract, consider limiting yourself to these topics:

- The problem area and need for additional research in the area.
- Research purposes, questions, or hypotheses and their importance.
- Relationship to the literature.
- The type of research being proposed.
- Types of implications that might result from the findings.

Example 1 covers these elements in a short abstract.

Example 1

Historically, African American churches have played a central role as a provider of human services within a healing community. At the present time, however, we do not know how well African American churches in economi-

cally depressed urban communities are serving this historic function. The purpose of the proposed research is to fill this gap in the literature. Specifically, a telephone survey of African American clergy in one northeastern urban area will be conducted to determine levels of human support services provided by the churches and the extent to which the clergy make referrals to human service programs in the community. The resulting data will have implications for how clergy and human service program providers can cooperate in the delivery of services.[1]

When only a very short abstract is permitted, details on sampling, measurement, and methods of analysis may need to be omitted. If a long abstract is required or permitted, consider using subheadings to guide your readers. Example 2 shows a typical set of subheadings.

Example 2

Problem area (including importance)
Research purpose (or question or hypothesis)
Related literature (brief overview of most salient aspects)
Participants (including sampling plan)
Instrumentation (types of instruments that will be used; names of instruments are usually not needed in the abstract)
Method of analysis (descriptive and inferential, if any)
Potential implications

If you are writing a long abstract, be careful that it does not get so long that it becomes a burden on someone who is

---

[1] This example is loosely based on the work of Williams, D. R., Griffith, E. E. H., Young, J. L., Collins, C., & Dodson, J. (1999). Structure and provision of services in Black churches in New Haven, Connecticut. *Cultural Diversity and Ethnic Minority Psychology, 5,* 118-133.

examining it only to obtain an overview
of your proposed research.

Exercise for Topic 45

1. Are you required to write a short abstract? If so, how many words are permitted?

2. Will you be writing a long abstract? If so, will you be using subheadings?

3. Write the first draft of an abstract for your proposal.

Topic 46

Developing a Timeline

Many novice researchers seriously underestimate the amount of time that it will take them to conduct and write up their research. Thus, it is important to draw up a timeline and get feedback on it from experienced researchers. This is especially important for thesis and dissertation students since timelines will allow members of their committees to comment on whether they are realistic, not only in terms of the students' time, but also in terms of the restraints on their own time as committee members.

All researchers should build into their timelines adequate time for others to review their work as it progresses as well as when the first draft of the final research report is completed. Thesis and dissertation students should also consult with their chair regarding whether the chair wants to review all written materials *before* other committee members are given copies. If so, additional time will be needed to allow for a two-stage review of each part of the research report.

Example 1 shows a sample timeline submitted by one student. Keep in mind that timelines can vary dramatically depending on the circumstances of the research. For instance, in this case, the student prepared a preliminary literature review for the proposal and will need to complete it. Other students may have written a complete literature review while preparing their proposals. Also, this student was employed full-time and could devote only evenings and weekends to conducting the research.

Example 1

1. Complete literature review. (one month)
2. Have literature review reviewed by the thesis chair. (two weeks) Have literature review reviewed by other committee members. (two more weeks)
3. Obtain mailing lists from University Data Center. (two weeks)
4. Prepare survey cover letter and first draft of questionnaire. (one week)
5. Have cover letter and questionnaire reviewed by committee chair. (one week)
6. Pilot test cover letter and questionnaire and revise. (one week)
7. Have revised cover letter and questionnaire reviewed by thesis chair. (two weeks) Have them reviewed by other committee members. (two more weeks)
8. Write the Method section of the research report. (two weeks)
9. Have the Method section reviewed by the thesis chair. (two weeks) Have it reviewed by other committee members. (two more weeks)
10. Mail letter and questionnaire and wait for responses. (three weeks)
11. Mail follow-up questionnaire, and wait for responses. (two weeks)
12. Tabulate responses. Conduct descriptive and inferential analyses. (two weeks)
13. Write the Results and Discussion sections of the research report. (two weeks)
14. Have the Results and Discussion sections reviewed by the thesis chair. (two weeks) Have them reviewed by other committee members. (two more weeks)
15. Assemble the first draft of the complete report. Have it reviewed by an instructor at the University Writing Center for mechanical flaws in grammar, punctuation, etc. (one week)

16. Submit the complete first draft (revised in light of Step 15) to the committee chair and the committee members for their review. (two weeks)
17. Rewrite and revise in light of Step 16 and resubmit for feedback. (two weeks)
18. Make final changes based on Step 17. (one week)
19. Format the thesis and submit it to the University Librarian for format approval. (one week)
20. Take a vacation in Hawaii!

If you have sufficient time, you may be able to shorten the total time by engaging in overlapping activities. For example, while your committee is reviewing your literature review, you might begin writing your questionnaire. If so, prepare a graphic timeline such as the one shown here (in part) in Example 2.

Example 2

Graphic Timeline for Completion of Research (Partial)	Jan.	Feb.
1. Complete literature review	XXXXXXXXXXXX	
2. Have literature review reviewed by chair		XXXXX
3. Have literature review reviewed by other committee members		XXXXXX
4. Obtain mailing list from University Data Center		XXXXXX
5. Prepare survey cover letter and first draft of questionnaire		XXX

Note: XXX = one week; XXXXXX = two weeks; and so on.

Exercise for Topic 46

1. Prepare a timeline for your proposed research.

Part K

Sample Research Proposals for Discussion

In this part of the book, you will find two sample proposals for (1) a survey and (2) an experiment. Both are solid proposals. However, expectations for proposals vary according to purpose. For example, a proposal written as a term project in a research methods class may be acceptable with less detail than one written for dissertation research. Thus, these proposals are presented to be used as starting points for discussion in class. For instance, instructors can discuss which parts of each proposal meet his or her expectations for the proposals students will be writing. In addition, after reading them, students may raise questions about how they might serve as models for their own work.

Notes

Sample Proposal 1

Gender Differences in Sexual Abuse Outcomes and Recovery Experiences: A Survey of Therapist-Survivors[1]

A Research Proposal Based on the Work of

Liza Little and Sherry L. Hamby[2]
University of New Hampshire

Abstract

If gender differences in recovery from childhood sexual abuse (CSA) go unrecognized, treatment may be unsuccessful. At the current time, most of the established methods for treating CSA are based primarily on work with female victims. In addition, there is growing interest in the role that mental health professionals' own traumas play in their treatment of others. This proposed study will survey by mail more than 1,000 professionals in one state regarding their own CSAs. It is anticipated that more than 100 will report a CSA history. These will be asked to respond to questions regarding the abuse characteristics, outcomes, and recovery experiences. Differences between men and women will be tested for statistical significance. The results will have implications for both training mental health professionals and for practicing clinicians who work with clients with CSAs.

Introduction and Literature Review

Working with victims of childhood sexual abuse (CSA) can be challenging and demanding. The challenges can be even greater when working with male survivors because most interventions have been developed largely from helping female survivors. This situation exists because more women present as CSA victims or disclose such histories in treatment. Men are still often viewed as perpetrators, not victims, and it is only recently that the paucity of services tailored for male victims has been addressed (Mendel, 1995). Many clinicians are increasingly beginning to appreciate that male and female survivors tend to be different from one another in important ways (Becker-Lausen & Mallon-Kraft, 1995; Feiring, Taska, & Lewis, 1996; Hunter, 1991; Krugman, 1996; Orbuch, Harvey, Davis, & Merbach, 1994; Rew, Esparza, & Sands, 1991).

---

[1]This proposal was adapted from this report of completed research: Little, L. & Hamby, S. L. (1999). Gender differences in sexual abuse outcomes and recovery experiences: A survey of therapist-survivors. *Professional Psychology: Research and Practice, 30,* 378–385. Copyright © 1999 by the American Psychological Association, Inc. Reprinted with permission. The material from the beginning of the article up to the heading "Method" is unabridged from the original. The remainder of the proposal as well as the abstract was modified from the original with permission of the authors.

[2]LIZA LITTLE is a clinical psychologist and an assistant professor of nursing at the University of New Hampshire. She is currently doing research on health care workers' workplace violence and the effect childhood abuse history has on it. SHERRY L. HAMBY is a research associate at the Family Research Laboratory, University of New Hampshire, and a visiting scientist at the Arizona Prevention Center of the University of Arizona. She studies nonstranger victimization and is currently working on issues of intervening against interpersonal violence in diverse cultural settings. Correspondence concerning the article on which this proposal is based should be addressed to Liza Little, Department of Nursing, University of New Hampshire, Hewitt Hall, Durham, NH 03824. Electronic mail may be sent to LLittle @ hopper.unh.edu

A number of critical questions for the practicing therapist remain unanswered, however (Hunter, 1991; Kendall-Tackett & Simon, 1992; Orbuch et al., 1994). These questions include the following: How are patterns of abuse different for men and women? Do men and women have different long-term outcomes? How do male and female survivors work on their healing? What ways do they find are most important for their healing? What are the treatment implications of any gender differences? The lack of answers to these basic questions leaves the practicing clinician with the dilemma of knowing that male and female survivors are often affected by CSA in different ways but having no guidance about how to address those differences in treatment. This article explores gender differences in CSA histories and the perceived helpfulness of a variety of recovery experiences among therapists who are survivors of CSA.

What Are the Known Gender Differences in CSA and Why Do They Exist?

One of the best documented gender differences is the lower reported incidence of CSA among males than females (e.g., Finkelhor, Hotaling, Lewis, & Smith, 1990; Little & Hamby, 1996). In many studies, females report CSA victimization at a rate two to three times higher than do males. This higher level of reporting is likely to be one reason that female victims have been studied more than male victims, but there are still significant numbers of male victims. What is more, male victims may be underidentified in treatment settings because of the following variables noted by Holmes, Offen, and Waller (1997): (a) Males may be differently affected by their abuse than females, (b) men who have been abused enter the system at different points than women do and are less frequently seen in clinical settings as opposed to criminal settings, (c) men tend not to disclose their abuse, and (d) clinicians fail to ask about abuse histories with male clients.

Many areas are negatively affected for both male and female survivors, including self-esteem, relationship functioning, coping, and sexual adjustment (Hunter, 1991; Orbuch et al., 1994; Rew et al., 1991; Kelly, McDonald, & Waterman, 1987). Despite some similarities, however, important gender differences have been found. Male victims, as compared with female victims, are more likely to have identity conflicts and to ruminate (Hunter, 1991), to have greater difficulties coping and handling relationships (Orbuch et al., 1994; Rew et al., 1991), and to have a less complete understanding of the assault and less success in account making (Orbuch et al., 1994). Male survivors may also exhibit more externalizing behaviors involving aggression and acting out (Becker-Lausen & Mallon-Kraft, 1995; Krugman, 1996). Societal differences in gender roles may also play a part. Several studies suggest that men are less likely to report abuse because of cultural biases that discourage acknowledgment of vulnerability and help seeking and that encourage the minimization of emotional pain (Boyd & Beail, 1994; Gordon, 1990; Holmes et al., 1997; Krugman, 1996; Lew, 1990). Sociocultural bias may also lead men to describe CSA experiences more positively than female victims and to report that they enjoy even very early sexual experiences (Finkelhor, 1979; Fromuth & Burkhart, 1989).

Other effects of CSA that may be more specific to male victims include the development of confusion in adult sexual orientation (Dhaliwal, Gauzas, Antonowicz, & Ross, 1996). Men are much more likely than women to be abused by same-sex perpetrators. For example, in Finkelhor et al.'s national study (1990), only 2% of female victims reported that their perpetrator was of the same sex, whereas 83% of men identified a same-sex perpetrator. Thus, it is possible that issues related to homosexuality may be more common among male sexual abuse victims. It has been suggested that a male who is victimized by a male perpetrator may come to feel that he was picked because he has certain qualities of homosexual individuals (Finkelhor, 1979). This model, however, has not been substantiated by current empirical studies (Dhaliwal et al., 1996; Hunter, 1991). Others suggest that males abused by male perpetrators may become fearful of becoming homosexual and become irrationally afraid of being identified by themselves or others as homosexual (Gilgun & Reiser, 1990; Hunter, 1991). This fear has also been cited as a reason why men may be more reluctant to disclose their abuse histories. These notions also need further empirical substantiation, however.

In contrast, women may blame themselves more and be more prone to feeling shame about their abuse experiences than men (Feiring et al., 1996; Lewis, 1992). Women more frequently report body disturbance problems (Hunter, 1991) and internalizing symptoms, such as depression and anxiety (Becker-Lausen & Mallon-Kraft, 1995; Krugman, 1996). Others suggest that girls may be more at risk for making internal negative attributions about the abuse (Feiring et al., 1996). Current popular psychology has promoted the idea that sexual abuse is a major source of life difficulties for many women, so they may attribute more of their difficulties to sexual abuse than do men.

Recovery from CSA

There is scant empirical literature on recovery from CSA (Beutler & Hill, 1992). One empirical study of a small group of female survivors found that self-reports of good adjustment were attributed to extra-familial support, high self-esteem, spirituality, and stable interpersonal relationships (Valentine & Feinauer, 1993). In a rare study comparing recovery for males and females, Orbuch et al. (1994) found that women who make sense out of their assault by talking about the experience with someone close to them report more success in coping and greater resolution of the experience. This same study found that males had engaged in fewer recovery strategies than females. These studies and recent clinical literature suggest that recovery from abuse should be conceptualized as a multidimensional process. This process includes working through individual issues, engaging in formal help seeking, and identifying and using relational and vocational supports (Harvey, 1996; Herman, 1994; Matsakis, 1994; Morrow & Smith, 1995; Roth & Newman, 1993). Recovery for survivors may best be viewed as a process that includes positive family and interpersonal functioning and community involvement as well as traditional therapy (Harvey, 1996; Hill & Alexander, 1993; Valentine & Feinauer, 1993). What past studies have not indicated, however, is whether some of these experiences are more healing for females or males. If such gender differences exist, they imply that treatment planning should take client gender into consideration.

Healing the Healer: Recovery Issues for Therapists with CSA Histories

Therapists also may grow up in dysfunctional families, although exact estimates of this vary across studies (Sherman, 1996). Previous data on CSA prevalence suggest that rates among clinicians are generally comparable to those found for community samples. Estimated CSA rates from past studies of mental health providers range from 6% to 43% (Little & Hamby, 1996), with most clustering near the figure of 26% for women and 16% for men found in one major nationally representative study (Finkelhor et al., 1990). These estimates suggest that a significant number of providers have CSA histories.

There is a growing interest in the role that clinicians' own personal traumas play in their treatment of others because of the many high-risk situations that arise in the treatment of abused clients and the possibility of biases that might decrease one's effectiveness as a therapist (Elliott & Guy, 1993; Little & Hamby, 1996; Pearlman & MacIan, 1995; Sherman, 1996; Wilson & Lindy, 1994). As a provider, it may be hard to sincerely advocate a therapeutic technique or resource—for either a male or female victim—that one has personally found unsatisfying. Because of their training, therapists will have a keen understanding of differences among types of healing strategies and a perceptive awareness of what healing strategies they have personally undertaken. Thus, this population can be a particularly beneficial one with which to begin the study of healing processes and is potentially a source of new insights into gender-sensitive treatment. Identifying the most successful recovery experiences of therapist-survivors may also help shed light on the training and supervision needs of other providers with similar trauma histories. The purpose of this project is to compare male and female therapists with CSA histories on the characteristics of their abuse, the long-term outcomes of their abuse, and the saliency of various recovery experiences that have been helpful to their healing.

Method

Participants

The initial sample will consist of the 1,251 mental health professionals who belong to the Vermont Psychological Association, Vermont Association of Mental Health Counselors, Vermont Association of Social Workers, Vermont Association of Psychiatric Nurse Practitioners, and the Vermont Psychiatric Association. This sampling frame will be used because of the availability of mailing lists with current addresses from these associations. These mental health professionals will be mailed a questionnaire. For additional details, see "Procedures" below.

Instrumentation

Data for this study will be collected via a questionnaire that will solicit the following information.

Demographics and professional credentials. The questionnaire will begin by asking respondents to report their gender, age, highest degree (e.g., B.A., Ph.D.), and whether they are licensed.

Abuse History. Respondents will be asked whether they had ever been sexually abused. To establish a common ground for responding to this question, the questionnaire will provide this definition of sexual abuse, which is slightly modified from Finkelhor (1979):

> Sexual activity (contact and noncontact) involving a child (16 and under), with or without coercion, that you considered abusive.

The nature and extent of the abuse will also be assessed in questions about physical contact (whether abuse involved physical or no physical contact), frequency (whether the sexual abuse involved single or multiple contacts), and perpetrator relationship (whether the CSA involved a family member, stranger, or known but unrelated person).

Problems in family of origin. Respondents will be asked about the frequency of problems in their family of origin, but not asked to specify who in their family had the problem. The list of problems will include: divorce, alcoholism, mental illness, suicide, marital violence, and childhood physical abuse.

Negative outcomes. Regarding outcomes, the questionnaire will ask respondents to what extent 11 domains of their lives had been negatively affected specifically by their experience with CSA. They will be asked to rate each life area using a 5-point rating scale ranging from 5 (*not at all negatively affected*) to 1 (*extremely negatively affected*). The areas that will be listed are: relationship with significant others, relationship with my own kids, body image, self-esteem and sense of worthiness, ability to trust others, ability to cope with stress adequately, sexual satisfaction, maintaining healthy eating habits, maintaining healthy alcohol and drug habits, ability to maintain clear boundaries with others, and work. All of these questions will be reviewed by experts and pretested in a pilot study.

Healing experiences. Respondents will be given a list of 21 possible healing experiences and will be asked to rate each one's degree of importance to their recovery from their abuse. These ratings will be done on a 5-point scale from 5 (*extremely important*) to 1 (*not at all important*). Participants will also be able to rate a healing experience as "not applicable" because there may be some experiences that respondents will not have had such as having children or being hospitalized.

In preparation for this proposed research, clinical experts in the field of CSA were asked to sort through the list of 21 healing experiences and place them in groups or clusters. Four clusters emerged, which are indicated in italics as follows. *Working-through variables*: talking about the abuse to others, relinquishing my guilt, experiencing my feelings about what happened, confronting the perpetrator or those involved, identifying and gaining control over self-destructive and self-defeating behaviors, writing about what happened to me, and renegotiating relationships with family of origin. *Help resources*: undergoing personal therapy, undergoing family or couples therapy, joining a support group, being hospitalized, attending workshops to address my own recovery issues, and reading about abuse. *Career resources*: engaging in professional writing, taking part in community activism, attending workshops and conferences on CSA, becoming a therapist, being able to help other survivors, and writing about abuse. *Relational resources*: having a sense of religion or spirituality, having my own children, and having a loving relationship with my partner or friend.

Open-ended question: An open-ended question asking respondents to provide other comments will be included at the end of the questionnaire.

Procedure

During the first week of September 2001, the mental health professionals who belong to the associations mentioned above will be mailed a questionnaire accompanied by a cover letter and a stamped return envelope. The cover letter will inform respondents that the survey concerns issues of CSA and the experiences of professionals working with these issues. It will invite each professional to fill out the questionnaire even if he or she is not treating CSA clients.

In anticipation of a response rate substantially below 100%, which is characteristic of surveys conducted by mail, approximately three weeks after the initial mailing, a follow-up postcard and questionnaire will be sent to the entire sample. Note that because the responses will be anonymous, it will not be possible to send the follow-up to only those who failed to respond to the first mailing. The follow-up will ask those who responded earlier to ignore the second mailing. Based on the experiences of other researchers who have conducted surveys of professionals by mail with a follow-up, we anticipate a final response rate of 40% or more. Because the purpose of this research is to compare male and female therapists who have CSA histories, the responses of only those reporting such histories will be analyzed for the study.

Analysis

For *demographics* and *professional credentials*, percentages for the entire sample will be computed (e.g., percentage who are men and percentage who are women). These percentages will provide readers of the research report with an overview of the sociodemographics of the sample.

For *abuse history* and *problems in family of origin*, percentages will be calculated separately for women and men. Statistical tables will be prepared in which the percentages for men and women will be listed in separate columns, which will help readers compare the two groups. Gender differences will be tested for statistical significance with chi square tests using a probability level of .05 or less.

For *negative outcomes* and *healing experiences*, means and standard deviations will be computed separately for men and women. Because these variables will be measured on a 5-point scale, the means will be able to vary from 1 to 5. The differences between the means for men and for women will be tested for statistical significance with two-tailed t tests using a probability level of .05 or less. If Levene's test for equality of variance indicates unequal variances for any comparisons, the values of t will be adjusted accordingly. Statistical tables will be prepared in which the means, standard deviations, and values of t will be displayed.

For the *open-ended question*, responses will be examined to determine if there are distinct differences in the quality of the responses between men and women. If these are found, they will be described and illustrated with quotations from the respondents.

Discussion

Certain limitations of the proposed study should be acknowledged. First, the survey will not address recovery from all aspects. For instance, the survey will not address many characteristics of the abuse, personality variables of the survivors, or issues such as resiliency, all of which might affect a person's appraisal of the importance of various recovery variables. In addition, the survey will not explore gender differences with respect to same-sex perpetrators (Duncan & Williams, 1996). In addition, it is quite possible that the proposed sample for the current study, drawn entirely from Vermont, will not be representative of abused mental health professionals in general. Furthermore, ethnic and regional differences will not be explored within this proposed study. Thus, although the sample in this study will shed light on issues that affect respondents, it is limited in its generalizability to the general population of mental health professionals. Hence, this study should be viewed as exploratory and will need replication.

While recognizing the limitations of this study, we believe that the results may have important implications for consideration by mental health professionals. First, if significant differences are found between men and women, such professionals should explore their assumptions about male and female victims and avoid a one-size-fits-all mentality. They will need to be sensitive to the fact that most of the established methods for treating CSA are based primarily on work with female victims.

In addition, the results of this study will shed light on whether gender should play a role in the recommendation of therapeutic activities, keeping in mind that individual men and women may have preferences that are different from those suggested by traditional gender roles.

Next, it is important that graduate and postgraduate training programs take heed of the number of mental health professionals with CSA histories and design training for the treatment of abused clients that takes the trainee's personal history and gender into account. This proposed research will provide data that might be helpful in this effort.

Finally, the management and treatment of CSA pose complex and sometimes Herculean issues for professionals. We hope that the proposed research will help clarify the types of gender differences that may arise in treatment of CSA and contribute to the development of appropriate gender-sensitive strategies.

References

Becker-Lausen, E., & Mallon-Kraft, S. (1995, July). *Pandemic outcomes: The intimacy variable.* Paper presented at the 4th International Family Violence Research Conference, Durham, NH.

Betcher, R. W. (1996, March). *Men's modes of intimacy: Sports.* Paper presented at Men: The Challenges/Being a Patient—Being a Therapist Conference, Boston, MA.

Beutler, L., & Hill, C. (1992). Process and outcome research in the treatment of adult victims of CSA: Methodological issues. *Journal of Consulting and Clinical Psychology, 60,* 204–217.

Boyd, J., & Beail, N. (1994). Gender issues in male sexual abuse. *Clinical Psychology Forum, 64,* 35–38.

Dhaliwal, G., Gauzas, L., Antonowicz, D., & Ross, R. (1996). Adult male survivors of childhood sexual abuse: Prevalence, sexual abuse characteristics, and long-term effects. *Clinical Psychology Review, 16,* 619–639.

Duncan, L. E., & Williams, L. M. (1996, August). Gender role socialization and child sexual abuse of boys. Presented in S. L. Hamby (Chair), *Theorizing about gender socialization and power in family violence.* Symposium conducted at the 104th Annual Convention of the American Psychological Association, Toronto, Ontario, Canada.

Elliott, D., & Guy, D. (1993). Mental health professionals versus non-mental health professionals: Childhood trauma and adult functioning. *Professional Psychology: Research and Practice, 24,* 83–90.

Feiring, C., Taska, L., & Lewis, M. (1996). A process model for understanding adaptation to sexual abuse: The role of shame and defining stigmatization. *Child Abuse and Neglect, 20,* 767–782.

Finkelhor, D. (1979). *Sexually victimized children.* New York: Free Press.

Finkelhor, D., Hotaling, G., Lewis, I. A., & Smith, C. (1990). Sexual abuse in a national survey of adult men and women: Prevalence characteristics and risk factors. *Child Abuse and Neglect, 14*, 19–28.

Fromuth, M. E., & Burkhart, B. R. (1989). Long-term psychological correlates of childhood sexual abuse in two samples of college men. *Child Abuse and Neglect, 13*, 533–542.

Gilgun, J. F., & Reiser, E. (1990). The development of sexual identity among men sexually abused as children. *Families in Society, 71*, 515–523.

Gordon, M. (1990). Males and females as victims of childhood sexual abuse: An examination of the gender effect. *Journal of Family Violence, 5*, 321–331.

Harvey, M. (1996). An ecological view of psychological trauma and trauma recovery. *Journal of Traumatic Stress, 9*, 3–23.

Herman, J. (1994). *Trauma and recovery.* New York: Basic Books.

Hill, C., & Alexander, P. (1993). Process research in the treatment of adult victims of CSA. *Journal of Interpersonal Violence, 8*, 415–425.

Himelein, M., & McElrath, J. V. (1996). Resilient child sexual abuse survivors: Cognitive coping and illusion. *Child Abuse and Neglect, 20*, 747–758.

Holmes, G., Offen, L., & Waller, G. (1997). See no evil, hear no evil, speak no evil: Why do relatively few male victims of childhood sexual abuse receive help for abuse-related issues in adulthood? *Clinical Psychology Review, 17*, 69–88.

Hunter, J. (1991). A comparison of the psychosocial maladjustment of adult males and females sexually molested as children. *Journal of Interpersonal Violence, 6*, 205–219.

Kelly, R., McDonald, T., & Waterman, S. (1987). *Male abuse victims.* Unpublished data.

Kendall-Tackett, K., & Simon, A. (1992). A comparison of the abuse experiences of male and female adults molested as children. *Journal of Family Violence, 7*, 57–63.

Krugman, S. (1996, March). *Traumatic arousal in men.* Paper presented at Men: The Challenges/Being a Patient—Being a Therapist Conference, Boston, MA.

Lew, M. (1990). *Victims no longer: Men recovering from incest and other childhood sexual abuse.* New York: Harper & Row.

Lewis, M. (1992). *Shame: The exposed self.* New York: Free Press.

Little, L., & Hamby, S. L. (1996). The impact of a clinician's sexual abuse history, gender and theoretical orientation on treatment issues of childhood sexual abuse. *Professional Psychology: Research and Practice, 27*, 1–9.

Matsakis, A. (1994). *Post-traumatic stress disorder: A complete guide to treatment.* Oakland, CA: New Harbinger.

Mendel, M. P. (1995). *The male survivor: The impact of sexual abuse.* London: Sage.

Morrow, S., & Smith, M. L. (1995). Constructions of survival and coping by women who have survived childhood sexual abuse. *Journal of Counseling Psychology, 42*, 24–33.

Orbuch, T., Harvey, J., Davis, S., & Merbach, N. (1994). Account-making and confiding as acts of meaning in response to sexual assault. *Journal of Family Violence, 9*, 249–264.

Ostertag, P. A., & McNamara, J. R. (1991). "Feminization" of psychology: The changing sex ratio and its implications for the profession. *Psychology of Women Quarterly, 15*, 349–369.

Pearlman, L. A., & MacIan, P. S. (1995). Vicarious traumatization: An empirical study of the effects of trauma work on trauma therapists. *Professional Psychology: Research and Practice, 26*, 558–565.

Rew, L., Esparza, D., & Sands, D. (1991). A comparative study among college students of sexual abuse in childhood. *Archives of Psychiatric Nursing, 5*, 331–340.

Roth, S., & Newman, E. (1993). The process of coping with incest for adult survivors: Measurement and implications for research. *Journal of Interpersonal Violence, 8*, 363–377.

Shay, J. P. (1996, March). *Okay, I'm here, but I'm not talking! Psychotherapy with the reluctant male.* Paper presented at Men: The Challenges/Being a Patient—Being a Therapist Conference, Boston, MA.

Sherman, M. (1996). Distress and professional impairment due to mental health problems among psychotherapists. *Clinical Psychology Review, 17*, 299–315.

Valentine, L., & Feinauer, L. L. (1993). Resilience factors associated with male survivors of CSA. *American Journal of Family Therapy, 24*, 216–224.

Wilson, J., & Lindy, J. (1994). *Countertransference in the treatment of PTSD.* New York: Guilford Press.

Notes

Sample Proposal 2

A Comparison of Cooperative Learning, Interactive Multimedia, and Independent Study as Supplements to Distance Education Lectures[1]

A Research Proposal Based on the Work of

Nancy C. Boling
Department of Technology in Education, Mississippi State University

Daniel H. Robinson
Department of Educational Foundations, University of Louisville

Abstract

Distance education is the "fastest growing form of domestic and international education" (M. S. McIsaac & C. N. Gunawardena, 1996, p. 403). Unfortunately, research investigating effective use of distance education has not kept pace with implementation. In this study, the researchers will evaluate how lecture-based distance education can best be supplemented. Undergraduate volunteers will listen to a distance education lecture and then participate in one of three post-distance-education activities: cooperative learning, interactive multimedia, or a control condition of independent study. Participants will be tested on knowledge of material and will be asked how much they enjoyed the overall learning experience (i.e., the combination of the distance education lecture and the post-lecture activity). The differences among the means will be tested for statistical significance at the .05 level. The study will yield results with important implications for distance educators.

Introduction and Literature Review

Higher education was once restricted to only a few locations (classrooms) and times (class periods). With increasing numbers of adult learners and the need for more affordable education choices (Wilson & Mosher, 1994), demands for educational opportunities have called for the creation of more convenient times and locations. One educational approach that has emerged to meet these needs is distance education, where the teacher and students are separated physically but are joined by a technologically based system that allows communication and education to occur (Ham, 1995). The proposed study will investigate how distance education may be effectively enhanced with post-lecture learning activities.

"Distance education, structured learning in which the student and instructor are separated by time and place, is currently the fastest growing form of domestic and international education" (McIsaac & Gunawardena, 1996, p. 403). Distance education has encompassed everything from correspondence courses to instructional audio or video tapes, or both, to cable television to telecommunications to compressed video

[1]This proposal was adapted from this report of completed research: Boling, N. C. & Robinson, D. H. (1999). Individual study, interactive multimedia, or cooperative learning: Which activity best supplements lecture-based distance education? *Journal of Educational Psychology*, *91*, 169–174. Copyright © 1999 by the American Psychological Association, Inc. Reprinted with permission. The material from the beginning of the article up to the heading "Method" is unabridged from the original. The remainder of the proposal as well as the abstract were modified from the original with permission of the authors. Correspondence about the original work may be addressed to Nancy C. Boling, Department of Technology in Education, Mississippi State University, Mississippi State, MS 39762. Electronic mail may be sent to ncbl@ra.msstate.edu

and audio systems (Froke, 1994; Gibson & Gibson, 1995). In simple terms, distance education is defined as "an organizational and technological framework for providing instruction at a distance.... When the teacher and student(s) are separated by geography, technology is used to bridge the gap" (Ham, 1995, p. 43). Recently, the generally accepted technology used to bridge the gap is video-based interactive instruction.

Traditional classroom educators who have not been trained in distance learning are often asked to teach distance education classes at their respective institutions. Most of them approach the task in much the same way as they would a traditional classroom situation. Although traditional techniques (lecture, chalkboard diagrams, slides, photographs, charts, and handouts) have their place in instruction, distance education introduces new challenges and several issues that may affect instruction such as determining appropriate clothing for video transmission to minimize distractions, developing more support materials and distributing them in a timely manner, ensuring test security, using available telecommunication technologies such as electronic mail and faxes during the instructional session, promoting student-teacher interaction using unfamiliar technology, and resolving technological emergencies at home and remote sites (Brodie, Bronson, Coble, & Gray, 1994; Gibson & Gibson, 1995; Office of Technology Assessment, 1989). After teaching for 2 years in a video conferencing environment, Lawrence (1995) noted some differences between traditional classroom teaching and teaching at a distance. First, there is visual contact but only with one site at a time. Simultaneous visual contact with all participants does not exist. Second, the video conferencing environment discourages the expansiveness and spontaneity allowed by the proverbial blackboard approach. As a result, visuals and graphics have to be prepared in advance. Because of these differences, Lawrence recommended that teaching in the video conferencing environment be modified at the very least.

Instead of focusing on what can be done to enhance the distance education lecture, in the proposed study we will explore ways in which the amount of learning and students' satisfaction with the overall distance education experience could be facilitated by using postlecture learning activities. McIsaac and Gunawardena (1996), in commenting on the current state of research on distance education, argued:

> It is time...to examine factors such as instructional design, learning and instructional theory, and theoretical frameworks in distance education, which when applied to learning, might account for significant differences in levels of performance. The questions that need to be asked are...how best to incorporate media attributes into the design of effective instruction for learning. (p. 421)

Dede (1989) has similarly suggested that investigating the utility of learning activities combined with lecture-based distance education is essential. We chose two postlecture learning activities: (a) interactive multimedia, which involves incorporating media attributes (e.g., Karraker, 1992), and (b) cooperative learning, which has received the strongest support from the research literature (e.g., Johnson & Johnson, 1996).

Interactive Multimedia

With the advent of computer-based interactive multimedia, education has become more exciting for students of all ages. Dramatic reading improvements, drastic reductions in absenteeism and dropout rates, and an impressive improvement of analytical reasoning skills were all attributed to involvement in interactive multimedia learning introduced into school systems in California, Florida, and Ohio (Karraker, 1992).

Because of the many stages of development that interactive multimedia has gone through in the last several years, it is important to know what is meant by the loosely used term. *Interactive multimedia* is digitally integrated, organized information that includes text, graphics, and still images such as photographs, animation, audio, and motion video in a user-friendly interface on the computer. It allows the user to navigate at will to find and view information (Dyrli & Kinnaman, 1995; Galbreath, 1994). It increases both the quality and quantity of information that can be exchanged between the computer and the user (D. I. Barker, 1994).

The benefits of multimedia instruction for both education and business include interactivity through its user interface and flexibility of obtaining instruction in reference to scheduling, self-pacing, retention, availability, and type of learning environment (Chen, 1994). However, multimedia does have its limitations. A huge amount of computer memory storage is required for digital video—as much as 22.5 megabytes of storage for 1 s of video. In addition, video needs to be compressed and decompressed in order for the computer to process the motion along with graphics and text. Often, unless there is a hardware solution, computer processing slows down, which results in unacceptable video motion or speed of animation (Chen, 1994). In higher education, interactive multimedia software development is difficult because, in many instances, educators, scholars, and publishers who know the course content cannot program the software. Likewise, many programmers are often poorly versed in educational theory or methods (Kalmbach, 1994).

Regardless of its advantages or disadvantages, multimedia in education is having a definite impact on the way students learn (Chen, 1994). At both the elementary (T. A. Barker & Torgesen, 1995; Foster, Erickson, Foster, Brinkman, & Torgesen, 1994) and college levels (Liu & Reed, 1995; Miketta & Ludford, 1995), instruction in a multimedia format has been found to be advantageous to traditional instruction.

Cooperative Learning

Johnson and Johnson (1996) described cooperative learning as involving the use of small groups in instructional environments where students work together to maximize their own and each others' learning. There are four types of cooperative learning: formal, informal, base groups, and academic controversy. Formal cooperative learning involves students working together from one class period to several weeks, whereas informal cooperative learning involves students working in temporary, ad hoc groups that last from a few minutes to one class period. Cooperative base groups combine students of mixed abilities for at least 1 year to provide support for cognitive and social progress. Finally, academic controversy groups are formed when students disagree on an issue. Two students in the group are assigned the "pro" position and two are assigned the "con" position. Students discuss, reverse perspectives, and then meet to resolve the controversy. In the present study, we will use informal cooperative learning because of the temporary nature of the experimental conditions.

In theory and practice, cooperative learning differs considerably from traditional classroom instruction (Sharan & Sharan, 1987). According to Johnson and Johnson (1996), the discipline of using cooperative groups involves positive interdependence, individual accountability, face-to-face promotive interaction, teaching members interpersonal and small-group skills, and structuring group processing. There is substantial evidence that students working cooperatively in small groups can master teacher-presented information better than students working on their own (Slavin, 1987). Students who participate in cooperative learning have outperformed students in traditional classrooms at the elementary (Stevens & Slavin, 1995), secondary (Nichols & Miller, 1994), and college levels (Franklin, Griffin, & Perry, 1994). In addition to increasing learning, cooperative learning has been shown to increase students' social skills (Stevens & Slavin, 1995) and perceptions of ability and valuing of content (Nichols & Miller, 1994) and to reduce students' anxiety (Keeler & Anson, 1995).

Given the increasing popularity of distance education combined with the lack of empirical research on its effective use, in the present study we will investigate whether students will benefit from participating in either cooperative learning or interactive multimedia activities after a distance education lecture. The procedures we will use for both the cooperative learning and interactive multimedia groups are based on what we believe usually happens in higher education classrooms. We simply want to see if either of these two learning activities will facilitate learning and lead to more satisfaction than typical individual study. We will give students in the individual study condition the same fact sheet as that given to the cooperative learning group. This sheet will contain the same information that will be presented in the interactive multimedia module to ensure that any differences will not be attributed to access to material. By doing this, we hope to avoid the pitfalls associated with some experimental learning studies that use "sit-in-the-closet-and-do-nothing" control conditions (Levin, 1994).

Method

Participants

Undergraduates enrolled in five classes offered in the Department of Health, Physical Education, Recreation, and Sport at Mississippi State University in the Deep South during the next semester will participate in the study for course credit. The five classes will be PE1223: Personal Health; PE1313: Introduction to Physical Education; PE1783: Introduction to Athletic Training; PE3283: Athletic Training Practicum I; and PE4233: Biomechanics. Although these are intact classes, students in each class will be asked to volunteer. Those who do so will be randomly assigned to one of the following groups: individual study group, cooperative learning group, or interactive multimedia group.

Instrumentation

The instruments will be a prequestionnaire, a postquestionnaire, a pretest, and a posttest. The tests will be developed under the guidance of the instructors whose classes will be involved in the study. The prequestionnaire will provide demographic information such as classification, sex, age, and students' previous experience with distance education, cooperative learning, interactive multimedia, and computers. On the postquestionnaire, students will be asked to rate their level of satisfaction for the overall session (combination of the distance education lecture and the postlecture activity). A 0 will indicate very dissatisfied and 5 will indicate very satisfied. The pretest will contain 25 multiple-choice items, each with three alternatives. Students will be instructed to circle the correct answer. The posttest will have the same questions as the pretest, except that the questions will be in a different, randomized order. A Kuder-Richardson reliability coefficient will be computed for both the pretest and posttest.

Materials

Several instructional materials will be used in the study. There will be assignment cards, a three-page fact sheet, a four-page worksheet, a four-page answer sheet, and an interactive multimedia learning module. The assignment cards will be 3 in. × 5 in. (7.62 cm × 12.7 cm) note cards containing information concerning classroom (group) assignment. One third of the cards (for the cooperative learning group) also will contain a number indicating the group in which each student will participate and the name of a role assigned to each group member—task master, researcher, checker, or recorder.

Students in the individual study and cooperative learning groups will receive a three-page fact sheet. It will paraphrase the information covered in the distance education lecture. Students in the cooperative learning group also will receive a four-page worksheet that contains 31 questions. Most of these will involve providing a short answer, making a list, or labeling a diagram. In addition to the worksheet, the checkers in each of the five cooperative learning groups will receive an answer sheet. The answer sheet will be a correctly completed worksheet.

Students in the interactive multimedia group will navigate through a computer-based multimedia module titled "Heart Disease—Are You Willing to Take the Risk?" To ensure that the three experimental groups will not differ in terms of their access to information, the interactive module will contain the same information as the three-page fact sheet. It will be developed by the first author who has had five years of experience in developing educational interactive multimedia modules. The module will be developed in HyperCard 2.3 and be reviewed by three instructors who previously taught hypermedia classes. It will be organized into eight sections: basic functions of the heart, smoking, hypertension, cholesterol, stress, heredity, exercise, and multiple risk factors.

The module will contain 57 color images (scanned or created), one color chart, 17 introductory or explanatory QuickTime movies containing computer-based audio and digital video (created with Adobe Premiere) or custom animations with audio (created with Macromedia Director), two specific requests for information interaction by the participants, at least six navigational buttons on each card with up to two additional menu buttons on other cards, and an interactive practice exam with immediate auditory and visual feedback. The practice exam will contain the same information as the worksheet given to the cooperative learning group.

Procedure

A preliminary meeting with the teachers of the five classes will be held in May to discuss the participation of the students in the study, the content of the distance education session, and procedures for incorporating this activity into their courses. Three weeks after classes begin for the fall semester, students will be informed of the study and be asked to provide informed consent to participate. They will be given the prequestionnaire and pretest. All of this will occur during the students' scheduled class time. Students will be able to choose to participate during one of the times indicated—6:00 to 8:00 p.m. on either a Tuesday or Wednesday night 2 weeks later.

On the chosen night, students will be seated in an electronic classroom. The distance lecture will be transmitted from an electronic conference room located in an adjacent building and will last approximately 25 min. This will emulate a true distance education learning situation in that there will be a remote site where the students will be located and a transmission site where the instructor will be located. Interaction will not be allowed at any time during the lecture. Students will be able to push a button to activate a microphone to ask or answer questions.

Before the lecture, assignment cards will be randomly shuffled by the researcher and distributed to students after the lecture. Six facilitators (two for each of the three treatment groups) will direct students and answer any questions that arise. The facilitators for each of the three groups will accompany their respective groups to the assigned classrooms. On arrival at the designated classrooms, the facilitators will give the students a 5-min break. After returning to the assigned classrooms, students will be given 5 min of instructions on the procedures to follow. The facilitators will be instructed not to teach any of the material that was covered in the lecture but only to assist the students with procedural questions. After the lead facilitator reads typed instructions to the group, students will be given 35 min to perform their particular learning activity and will then be administered the postquestionnaire for 10 min, followed by the posttest for 20 min. Students and classroom teachers will be debriefed on the purpose and findings of the study during their regular class periods two weeks after the data are collected.

Students in the individual learning condition will study the fact sheet and any notes that they may take during the lecture. Students in the cooperative learning condition will use an informal cooperative learning procedure as outlined by Johnson and Johnson (1994). Students will follow the guidelines of working cooperatively to achieve a joint learning goal in temporary ad hoc groups that will last for a short period of time. Although it is difficult to determine in advance whether the students will accept a mood conducive to learning or will focus on the material to be learned, they will each be required to complete the worksheets and turn them in as a group. Students will also receive a fact sheet and will be able to use any of their notes that they take during the lecture. Also, although the students will not help to set expectations for the class session, they will have to interpret the expectations required by the facilitators and fulfill those expectations. Students will be responsible for ensuring that others in their group learn and understand the material taught. This will be accomplished by assigning each student a certain role in his or her group. The roles will be read to the students by the lead facilitator as explained later in this section. The checker in the group will be given an answer sheet. Finally, students will obtain closure to an instructional session by completing and turning in the postquestionnaire and posttest.

After the lead facilitator reads the instructions, students will be assembled into the groups that are designated on the assignment cards. There will be about five groups with four students per group. Each of the four group members will be assigned a role with the instructions given by the facilitator and repeated in writing on the back of the assignment card. The four roles will be as follows. The task master will be instructed to focus the group's efforts on answering the questions on the worksheet. The researcher will be instructed to find the answer to any question in the fact sheet if it cannot be found either in students' notes or their copies of the fact sheet. The checker will be instructed to check the accuracy of the group's answers using the answer sheet, and the recorder will be instructed to make sure group members write the correct answer on their worksheets.

Students in the interactive multimedia condition will be assembled in a classroom equipped with Macintosh computers. The interactive multimedia module program will be active on each computer, and the two facilitators will be prepared to help with any technical problems. Students will be able to access information in the module in any order that they desire. If students want to first know about stress, they access the stress section of the module rather than smoking, which is the first risk factor covered in the module, the lecture, and the fact sheet.

Analysis

For the postquestionnaire item on overall satisfaction with the learning experience (where 0 = very dissatisfied and 1 = very satisfied), means and standard deviations will be computed for each group. A one-way ANOVA will be used to test the significance of the differences among the three means. If the overall ANOVA is statistically significant at the .05 level, Tukey's honestly significant difference test will be used to make multiple comparisons among pairs of means.

Assuming that the distributions of the scores on the 25-item multiple-choice pretest and posttest are not seriously skewed, the analysis of them will be conducted as follows. The means and standard deviations of the scores will be computed. If the assumption of homogeneity of regression slopes is supported, a one-way analysis of covariance will be conducted using the pretest as the covariate and the posttest as the dependent measure. If this assumption is not met, the students in each learning condition will be divided into two groups: (a) those who are above the median on the pretest and (b) those who are below the median forming six groups as shown in Table 1. A factorial analysis of variance using learning activity (individual study vs. cooperative learning vs. interactive multimedia) and pretest score (low vs. high scores as determined by scores below and above the median score) as between-subjects factors will be conducted. This will be used to determine the significance of the main effects and the interaction at the .05 level. Tukey's honestly significant difference test will be used to make any warranted multiple comparisons.

Table 1   *Means and standard deviations of posttest scores*

Pretest score	Cooperative learning			Interactive multimedia			Independent study		
Low (below median)	M =	SD =	n =	M =	SD =	n =	M =	SD =	n =
High (above median)	M =	SD =	n =	M =	SD =	n =	M =	SD =	n =

Discussion

In summary, distance education has been cited in the literature as one of the fastest growing forms of education, yet has been understudied. This proposed study will contribute to the literature on this topic by examining the effectiveness of three types of supplementary instructional activities for a distance education lecture. More than 100 students who will have received the lecture via distance education will be divided at random into three groups to participate in supplementary (post-distance learning) activities. One group of students will participate in interactive multimedia activities, another will participate in cooperative learning, and a third, the control group, will engage in independent study activities. Pre- and posttests will measure students' knowledge, and a questionnaire item will measure satisfaction with the overall learning process.

Two limitations of this study deserve mention. First, this experiment will be conducted with only volunteer students at one university in the Deep South. This will limit the external validity of the experiment, making it necessary to use caution in making generalizations to other college populations. Second, the study will examine only one health education lecture. It is possible that the findings of this study will not apply to other lectures in health education or to lectures in other academic disciplines.

Three strengths of the proposed study also deserve mention. First, students' satisfaction will be examined. Experiments on teaching and learning too often emphasize cognitive learning as an outcome to the exclusion of affective variables such as satisfaction with learning experiences. Without information on students' affective reactions, instructional delivery systems cannot be adequately assessed. Second, random assignment will be used to place students in one of the three treatment conditions. Thus, the study will be a true experiment with high internal validity. Finally, the administration of the learning conditions will be highly structured and controlled (as opposed to allowing instructors to implement various forms of supplementary instruction without explicit guidance). This structure and control will also contribute to the internal validity of the experiment and allow for a relatively unambiguous interpretation of the data.

In light of the data on student learning and satisfaction generated by this study, the researchers will discuss the implications for those who are administering and teaching in distance education programs. The most direct implications will relate to methods for supplementing and reinforcing material covered in distance education lectures.

References

Anderson-Inman, L., Horney, M. A., Chen, D. T., & Lewin, L. (1994). Hypertext literacy: Observations from the ElectroText project. *Language Arts, 71,* 279-287.

Barker, D. I. (1994). A technological revolution in higher education. *Journal of Educational Technology Systems, 23,* 155-168.

Barker, T. A. & Torgesen, J. K. (1995). An evaluation of computer-assisted instruction in phonological awareness with below average readers. *Journal of Educational Computing Research, 13,* 89-103.

Brodie, K., Bronson, J., Coble, J., & Gray, D. (1994, Fall). *Distance learning interactive classroom faculty guide.* A document for the Office of Continuing Education and Learning Resource Center, Chesapeake College, Wye Mills, Maryland. Available World Wide Web URL: http://www.chesapeake.edu/Dislearn/facguide.html

Chen, L. (1994). Digital multimedia instruction: Past, present, and future. *Journal of Educational Technology Systems, 23,* 169-175.

Corbett, A. T. & Anderson, J. R. (1991, April). *Feedback control and learning to program with the CMU Lisp Tutor.* Paper presented at the annual meeting of the American Educational Research Association, Chicago, IL.

Dede, C. (1989, July). The evolution of distance learning: Technology-mediated interactive learning. *Technologies for learning at a distance* (Science, Education, and Transportation Program for the Office of Technology Assessment). Washington, DC: Congress of the United States.

Dyrli, O. E. & Kinnaman, D. E. (1995). Part 4: Moving ahead educationally with multimedia. *Technology & Learning, 15* (7), 46-51.

Foster, K. C., Erickson, G. C., Foster, D. F., Brinkman, D., & Torgesen, J. K. (1994). Computer administered instruction in phonological awareness: Evaluation of the DaisyQuest program. *Journal of Research and Development in Education, 27,* 126-137.

Franklin, G., Griffin, R. & Perry, N. (1994). Effects of cooperative tutoring on academic performance. *Journal of Educational Technology Systems, 23,* 13-25.

Froke, M. (1994). A vision and promise: Distance education at Penn State part 1—toward an experienced-based definition. *Journal of Continuing Higher Education, 42*(2), 16-22.

Galbreath, J. (1994). Multimedia in education: Because it's there? *TechTrends, 39*(6), 17-20.

Gibson, C. & Gibson, L. (1995). Lessons learned from 100+ years of distance learning. *Adult Learning, 7,* 15.

Ham, R. (1995, March). Distance education: Teaching tools for the 21st century. *The Technology Teacher,* pp. 43, 45.

Hinkle, D. E., Wiersma, W. & Jurs, S. G. (1994). *Applied statistics for the behavioral sciences* (3rd ed.). Boston: Houghton Mifflin Company.

Johnson, D. W. & Johnson, R. T. (1994). *Learning together and alone* (4th ed.). Boston: Allyn and Bacon.

Johnson, D. W. & Johnson, R. T. (1996). Cooperation and the use of technology. In D. H. Jonassen (Ed.), *Handbook of research for educational communications and technology* (pp. 1017-1044). New York: Macmillan.

Kalmbach, J. A. (1994). Just in time for the 21st century: Multimedia in the classroom. *TechTrends, 39*(6), 29-32.

Karraker, R. (1992). Crisis in American education: Can multimedia save the day? *New Media, 2*(1), 23-27.

Keeler, C. M. & Anson, R. (1995). An assessment of cooperative learning used for basic computer skills instruction in the college classroom. *Journal of Educational Computing Research, 12,* 379-393.

Kinzie, M. B. (1990). Requirements and benefits of effective interactive instruction: Learner control, self-regulation, and continuing motivation. *Educational Technology, Research and Development, 38,* 5-21.

Land, S. M. & Hannifin, M. J. (1996). A conceptual framework for the development of theories-in-action with open-ended learning environments. *Educational Technology Research and Development, 44,* 37-53.

Lawrence, B. H. (1995). Teaching and learning via videoconference: The benefits of cooperative learning. *Journal of Educational Technology Systems, 24,* 145-149.

Levin, J. R. (1994). Crafting educational research that's both credible and creditable. *Educational Psychology Review, 6,* 231-243.

Liu, M. & Reed, W. M. (1995). The effect of hypermedia assisted instruction on second language learning. *Journal of Educational Computing Research, 12,* 159-175.

McIsaac, M. S. & Gunawardena, C. N. (1996). Distance education. In D. H. Jonassen (Ed.), *Handbook of research for educational communications and technology* (pp. 403-437). New York: Macmillan.

Miketta, J. B. & Ludford, D. (1995). Teaching with multimedia in the community college classroom. *T.H.E. Journal, 23,* 61-64.

Misanchuk, R. R. & Schwier, R. A. (1992). Representing interactive multimedia and hypermedia audit trails. *Journal of Educational Multimedia and Hypermedia, 1*(3), 355-372.

Nichols, J. D. & Miller, R. B. (1994). Cooperative learning and student motivation. *Contemporary Educational Psychology, 19,* 167-178.

Office of Technology Assessment. (1989). *Linking for learning. A new course for education* (ERIC Document Reproduction Service No. ED 310 765). Washington, DC: Congress of U.S.

Sharan, Y. & Sharan, S. (1987). Training teachers for cooperative learning, *Educational Leadership, 45*(3), 20-25.

Shute, V. J. & Regian, J. W. (1993). Principles for evaluating intelligent tutoring systems. *Journal of Artificial Intelligence in Education, 4,* 245-271.

Slavin, R. E. (1987). Cooperative learning and the cooperative school. *Educational Leadership, 45*(3), 7-13.

Stevens, R. J. & Slavin, R. E. (1995). The cooperative elementary school: Effects on students' achievement, attitudes, and social relations. *American Educational Research Journal, 32,* 321-351.

Wilson, J. M. & Mosher, D. N. (1994, June). *Interactive multimedia distance learning (IMDL): The prototype of the virtual classroom.* Paper presented at the meeting of the ED-MEDIA 94 World Conference, Vancouver, British Columbia, Canada. (ERIC Document Reproduction Service No. ED 388 303).

Table 1

Table of Recommended Sample Sizes (*n*) for Populations (*N*) with Finite Sizes[1]

N	*n*	*N*	*n*	*N*	*n*
10	10	220	140	1,200	291
15	14	230	144	1,300	297
20	19	240	148	1,400	302
25	24	250	152	1,500	306
30	28	260	155	1,600	310
35	32	270	159	1,700	313
40	36	280	162	1,800	317
45	40	290	165	1,900	320
50	44	300	169	2,000	322
55	48	320	175	2,200	327
60	52	340	181	2,400	331
65	56	360	186	2,600	335
70	59	380	191	2,800	338
75	63	400	196	3,000	341
80	66	420	201	3,500	346
85	70	440	205	4,000	351
90	73	460	210	4,500	354
95	76	480	214	5,000	357
100	80	500	217	6,000	361
110	86	550	226	7,000	364
120	92	600	234	8,000	367
130	97	650	242	9,000	368
140	103	700	248	10,000	370
150	108	750	254	15,000	375
160	113	800	260	20,000	377
170	118	850	265	30,000	379
180	123	900	269	40,000	380
190	127	950	274	50,000	381
200	132	1,000	278	75,000	382
210	136	1,100	285	100,000	384

[1]Adapted from: Krejcie, R. V. & Morgan, D. W. (1970). Determining sample size for research activities. *Educational and Psychological Measurement, 30,* 607–610.

Notes

Appendix A

Locating Literature Electronically*

Increasingly, students are being given direct access to electronic databases in academic libraries. In this topic, we will consider how to use them to locate articles in academic journals.

We will explore some of the important principles for locating literature electronically (via computer) from three major sources: (1) *Sociofile,* which contains the print versions of *Sociological Abstracts* and *Social Planning Policy & Development Abstracts,* covering journal articles published in over 1,600 journals; (2) PsycLIT, which contains the print version of *Psychological Abstracts,* with abstracts to journal articles worldwide since 1974;[1] and (3) *ERIC,* which contains abstracts to articles in education found in more than 600 journals from 1966 to date.[2] The following characteristics are true of all three databases.

First, for each journal article, there is a single *record;* a record contains all the information about a given article. Within each record, there are separate *fields* such as the title field, the author field, the abstract (that is, summary of the article) field, and the descriptor field.

A descriptor is a key subject-matter term; for example, *learning environments, learning disabilities,* and *learning theories* are descriptors in *ERIC.* One of the important ways to access the databases is to search for articles using appropriate descriptors. To determine which descriptors are available, each database has a *thesaurus.* It is important to refer to it to identify the terms you want to use in your search. For example, if your topic is *group therapy for child molesters,* the appropriate descriptors in PsycLIT are *group psychotherapy* and *pedophilia.*

The following are some principles for conducting a search. First, we can search a particular field or search entire records. If you have identified appropriate descriptors in the *thesaurus,* it is usually sufficient to search the descriptors fields using the descriptors.[3]

We may conduct a search for all articles containing either (or both) of two descriptors by using OR. For example, the instruction to find "dyslexia" OR "learning disabilities" will locate all articles with either one of these descriptors. Thus, using OR broadens our search.

We can also broaden our search by using a root word such as *alcohol* followed by an asterisk (*); the asterisk instructs the program to search for the plural form as well as derivatives such as *alcoholism* and *alcoholics.*

Frequently, we wish to narrow our search in order to make it more precise. An important instruction for doing this is AND. For instance, if we use the instruction to locate articles with *"learning environments* AND *dyslexia,"* the program will only identify articles with *both* these descriptors, and exclude articles that have only one of them.

We can also make our search more precise by using NOT. The instruction *"advertising* NOT *television"* will identify all articles relating to advertising but exclude any that relate to advertising on television.

If you are working in a field with thousands of references, you can be more precise by adding another search concept such as age group (child, adolescent, adult, or elderly) and population (human or animal).

If you are required to use only recent references, you can also limit the search to recent years.

---

*Reprinted with permission from Patten, M. L. (2000). *Understanding Research Methods: An Overview of the Essentials* (2nd ed.). Los Angeles: Pyrczak Publishing. Copyright © 2000 by Pyrczak Publishing. All rights reserved.

[1] Use the print version for journal articles published before 1974.

[2] The emphasis in this appendix is on journal articles. Note that PsycLIT also abstracts books, *Sociofile* also abstracts dissertations, and *ERIC* also abstracts unpublished documents such as convention papers, which are available on microfiche.

[3] If you are not able to find appropriate descriptors, conduct a "free text" search, using your own terms (such as *child molester,* which is not a *thesaurus* term) and searching entire records. If this term appears in any field in any of the records, the record(s) will be selected. If any are selected, examine the descriptors field to see what descriptors have been assigned to it—noticing *pedophilia,* you could now search again looking only in the descriptors field for the *thesaurus* descriptor, *pedophilia.*

Notes